Check It Off!

Check It Off!

Pave Your Way through College to Career

Vera Teller, Ph.D.

ROWMAN & LITTLEFIELD
Lanham • Boulder • New York • London

Published by Rowman & Littlefield
A wholly owned subsidiary of The Rowman & Littlefield Publishing Group, Inc.
4501 Forbes Boulevard, Suite 200, Lanham, Maryland 20706
www.rowman.com

Unit A, Whitacre Mews, 26-34 Stannary Street, London SE11 4AB

British Library Cataloguing in Publication Information Available

Library of Congress Cataloging-in-Publication Data

ISBN 978-1-4758-2954-9 (cloth : alk. paper)
ISBN 978-1-4758-2955-6 (paperback : alk. paper)
ISBN 978-1-4758-2958-7 (electronic)

∞™ The paper used in this publication meets the minimum requirements of American National Standard for Information Sciences—Permanence of Paper for Printed Library Materials, ANSI/NISO Z39.48-1992.

Printed in the United States of America

To my grandchildren, Dominic and Vincent:
Barriers are limitations in the mind. Pursue your dreams
and be happy. You are loved for who you are!

Contents

Foreword

I have been teaching at a state university level for 42 years. Over that time, I have prided myself in my ability and interest in working with my students with the overall goal of gaining the career that they desire. Sometimes it works and sometimes it doesn't. However, when it works, it is because the student is motivated and willing to do anything to succeed from the beginning. This book is about *you* getting the career you want and learning how to start toward that goal from day one at college. My experiences with more than 20,000 students over my career tell me that the students who start this way are the ones who meet their goal.

Too often I talk to senior students and ask them what they want to do when they graduate, and I hear, "I'm not really sure. I figure I will apply for some jobs and see what comes up." That is not a very good plan and often it fails.

Allow me to tell you about how one student of mine approached it differently. "Sienna" was a sophomore and a student in my class. When I talked about my research she seemed to be the most attentive student in the class and asked quite insightful questions for a 19-year-old. I mentioned our lab and she asked if she could join. I told her what I tell all students: come see me when you are starting your junior year and we will talk. Sienna was insistent and we compromised by me letting her sit in on a lab meeting. She never left and she is now completing her PhD and is certain to get a good job.

Dr. Teller's book is not one of those "self-help" books full of cute quizzes asking about what animal you most resemble or what cartoon character is most like you. It is full of valuable information set in a clear, orderly timetable where you build your skills and your persona across your four college years. You will learn about the value of finding a mentor (something dear to my heart) as well as how and why to keep a portfolio of your work starting at day one. You will hear about the value of public speaking, which, I believe, is the most important skill you will learn in school. We make our students present at many conferences and practice in front of us numerous times until they are comfortable and clear.

Dr. Teller will also tell you about the absolute importance of networking and even talk to you about how to communicate with those with whom you might want to work. She will tell you that college is more than coursework. It is a place to gather experiences and interests, and plan for your future.

Most importantly, she will tell you why your pursuit is "nonlinear." When I entered college I was going to be a professor of mathematics. I had my entire coursework planned out and knew exactly what was going to happen each year. That worked fine until I realized that I did not want to teach math to college students who, for the most part, were not interested. My nonlinear meanderings took me to several other disciplines that used math but were more "interesting" both to me and to my future students. I settled on psychology and never looked back.

Heed Dr. Teller's advice throughout this book. Start reading it *before* you go to your first day of college. Gain knowledge and gain experience. Visualize yourself being successful in four years and follow her plan to that success. But be open to the possibility that life might change.

You might not take the straight path you envisioned upon entering college. Your career goals may meander here and there but if you stay on task and follow her plan you will find a career that fits you and excites you. Mine has taken bizarre twists and turns even after I became a professor and now 42 years later I am still having the time of my life. I love my job, my colleagues, and my students, and this year I published my seventh book. I never thought I would publish a book but that is the path that opened up for me. Stay open and "Check It Off!" and you, too, will pave the way to a career that makes you happy and successful.

Dr. Larry D. Rosen
Professor Emeritus, Keynote Speaker, Research Consultant
California State University, Dominguez Hills
George Marsh Applied Cognition Laboratory

Preface

"Begin at the beginning," the King said, very gravely, "and
go on till you come to the end: then stop."

—Lewis Carroll, *Alice's Adventures in Wonderland*

Janet excelled in high school, was accepted to a top national college, and after graduation fell into a deep depression because she had no plans or direction for the future. It took a lot of time, resources, and doctors to get her back on her feet (literally) and on a path toward a career.

Once she "felt" better, she was able to start the career planning process. While at an informal gathering she was introduced to a woman who worked for an educational center similar to the Kaplan centers. Janet applied to the center upon hearing of a job opportunity. This was a perfect fit for her, because although the focus was on education, other aspects of the job would provide valuable experience. It provided an opportunity to gain experience in various areas: marketing, accounting, and business management. Also, part of the position was to discuss alternative approaches to educating special needs children to parents.

Within two years of working with children, Janet decided to pursue a master's degree in educational policy. After interning at the Department of Education in educational policy while attending school, she was offered a position at the department immediately after graduating.

Many books on the market advise college students on how to get a good job after college. *How to Find Fulfilling Work, The Worrier's Guide To Life, Homework for Grown-ups, A Short Guide to a Happy Life, God's Promises for Graduates, What Do I Do If...?, How to Change the World, The Path, Damn Good Advice, I Just Graduated Now What?, Paddle against the Flow, You are*

Not Special, and *Be Amazing* are a few books published at graduation time in 2015. *None of these books discuss the career process during college.*

Check It Off! Pave Your Way through College to Career engages YOU, the student, to participate in tasks fundamental to the career process while attending college. Therefore, you will be prepared at graduation to pursue a career.

Finding a job after college is more difficult in this day and age, especially, if you are not prepared. While most students *think* a college degree is the key to a great job, the professional landscape has changed. Businesses are looking for more: college graduates who have experience. A college education is more important as more technological and other skills are required. By managing your career through college, you be prepared to obtain a career after college. Don't wait until you graduate.

Changes in the economy affect how we view employment, in both seeking and securing a job. An employer was once a safe haven, providing security and safety to the individual and thus the extended family. As businesses have evolved, so must you. The continual process of acquiring new skills and becoming proficient in business functions is a must for the employee of tomorrow.

WHY COLLEGE?

Many students are questioning the need for going to college when others are emphasizing technical programs that don't require a college degree. There are still important reasons to attend college. The word itself implies different motivations; fundamentally, the goal of college is to educate, to prepare for a career, and to graduate. Four (or five) years in college is an opportunity to learn, meet other students, have fun, experience new ideas, have adventures, mature, and of course prepare for a career after college.

There seems to be a debate on what college is for. William Deresiewicz (2014) in his article in *The New Republic* stated,

> I taught many wonderful young people during my years in the Ivy League—bright, thoughtful, creative kids whom it was a pleasure to talk with and learn from. But most of them seemed content to color within the lines that their education had marked out for them. Very few were passionate about ideas. Very few saw college as part of a larger project of intellectual discovery and development.

Deresiewicz continued,

> The first thing that college is for is to teach you to think. That doesn't simply mean developing the mental skills particular to individual disciplines. Col-

lege is an opportunity to stand outside the world for a few years, between the orthodoxy of your family and the demands of career, and contemplate things from a distance.

Steven Pinker (2014) in his article from *The New Republic* stated,

> Educated people should be able to express complex ideas in clear writing and speech. They should appreciate that objective knowledge is a precious commodity, and know how to distinguish vetted fact from superstition, rumor, and unexamined conventional wisdom. They should know how to reason logically and statistically, avoiding the fallacies and biases to which the untutored human mind is vulnerable. They should think causally rather than magically, and know what it takes to distinguish causation from correlation and coincidence. They should be acutely aware of human fallibility, most notably their own, and appreciate that people who disagree with them are not stupid or evil. Accordingly, they should appreciate the value of trying to change minds by persuasion rather than intimidation or demagoguery.

College is a time for exploration, thinking out of the box, and discovering what you believe rather than what is expected. It is a time when you should question and discover.

EMBRACE OPPORTUNITIES

College is the time to take chances. If you ever wanted to take an acting class but never had the courage to attend, this is the time to make the effort. Tom regretted not joining the swim team in college. He loved the sport and took every swimming class the college offered. He rationalized not joining the team because he worked part-time. Yet, he would see the swim team practice and wished he was on that team.

Looking back, he was intimidated, lacked courage and self-confidence to try. His regret is that he didn't make the effort. He'll never know how good he was in comparison to others, or how good he could have become. It was a passion that he ignored.

> *Twenty years from now you will be more disappointed by the things you didn't do than by the ones you did do. So throw off the bowlines. Sail away from the safe harbour. Catch the trade winds in sails. Explore. Dream. Discover.*
>
> (*Mark Twain*)

Attending college offers so many opportunities and choices. Now is the time to embrace your passions. If you had dreams of going abroad, now is the time to take advantage of the study abroad program. If you love animals but never thought you could pursue a career in veterinary medicine, perhaps you might consider taking a part-time position in a veterinary office or volunteer at an animal rescue center. What people say to missed opportunities as they age is, "Woulda, coulda, shoulda." You don't want to be one of them. If you have a passion or an interest, college is the time to explore those opportunities.

John was a natural presenter and the college class was organized in a way to offer opportunities to give presentations. He had the ability to get up in front of a group of students and speak spontaneously. He was personable, interesting, and funny. He received positive feedback and encouragement from the students in the class. Because of the encouragement he received from the class, he is pursuing a career as a stand-up comic. He will complete his college education, but he is performing in various clubs in the area to pursue his passion.

Consider the four (or five) years in college—your time to explore and imagine. It is your time to take chances or risks. This is the time to experiment. If you are playing football but want to take a dance lesson…go for it! If you love to draw but think you are not that good, take a class. Experiment! Venture out. Take classes or join organizations that you have an interest in. This is what the college experience is all about.

CAREER AMBIVALENCE

Change is difficult for everyone. There are times when small changes happen, and then there are times when major changes occur. Transitioning from high school to college and then again from college to career are two such times. First, there is a huge focus on the student to get accepted to college. The emphasis is placed on good grades. Tests are taken in preparation to apply to colleges. In the senior year, college letters are sent to schools with the hope of getting accepted to the college of your choice.

Then, once in college, major changes occur; you have gone from being around people who are continually telling you what to do and when to do it, to, "You're on your own. Figure it out." This is where you fall back to what you do best; study and hang out with friends until you either drop out with the excuse, "I don't know what I want to do" or graduate with no plan on what you are going to do. *Few students know what they want to do when they enter college and pursue that career after college.*

Students leave college for many reasons. At times, many students feel lost navigating college. The numbers of students who enter two- or four-year colleges and leave without completing a degree are increasing (Cuseo, 2005). However, the reasons students stay in college to graduate are to prepare for an occupation (Astin, Parrot, Korn, & Sax, 1997) and college satisfaction (Noel & Levitz, 1995). Notice that students' remaining in college has very little to do with career choice or being undecided about a major. There are several studies by academics to support this statement (Lewallen, 1993, 1995).

However, many students enter college thinking they should know their career choice. It is common to *NOT* know. This is normal. Micceri (2002) studied students who changed majors and those who did not change. The students who changed majors displayed a higher rate of retention than those who did not change majors. Cuseo (2005) reported the following statistics:

- Three out of four students are uncertain about their career choices upon entry to college.
- Less than 10% of students who enter college with a major in mind feel that they know a great deal about their intended major.
- Uncertainty among new students increases rather than decreases during their first two years of college.
- Over two-thirds of entering students change their major during their first year.
- Fifty to seventy-five percent of all students who enter college with a declared major change their mind at least once before they graduate.
- Only one out of three seniors will major in the same field he or she preferred as a freshman.

The information to make decisions just doesn't happen. You don't wake up one morning and state, "I'm going to major in history and get a job in an art museum after college." Few students know their major and career choice. Even those who think they do can use a period of self-exploration and re-evaluation of a career decision.

Students should not rush to choose a major. First, discover yourself, and then find a major that will make you happy and want to learn.

THE COLLEGE EXPERIENCE

The academicians can debate the following questions: *What is college for? What is the return on investment for students on attending college compared with those who do not attend college?* The college years offer much for students, both academically and socially, and students should take advantage of the experience. Yet, for most students, the goal of college is to obtain a job once graduated. Most students don't have the financial background to take off after graduation for a year and travel through Europe. Most students move back home with their parents until a part-time job turns into a full-time position.

There is significant pressure on students to get a job right out of college. One student's parents wanted her to work full-time in lieu of attending college full-time to contribute to the family's income. The student indicated that there were many family discussions on earning money now, because the family perceived the value of education as a luxury.

Around the end of the third or beginning of the fourth year in college, panic sets in when someone asks, "What do you want to do when you graduate?" Then, all of a sudden you look back and say, those four years in high school and four years in college went extremely fast. At the end of the four years in college, you end up asking yourself, *"What am I going to do after college?"* Most students answer, "I don't know." Many students work so hard to get accepted to the college of their choice, to find that the four years in college went exceptionally fast, with no plan on what to do once they graduate. They are completely lost. The goal was to graduate from college and that was accomplished. Check! Done! Finished!

Parents too assume that the next step for their child upon graduation is to get a job. When that doesn't happen as quickly they think it should, they begin pressuring the child. Repeatedly, parents ask their child, "What do you plan on doing?" On one occasion, a mother screamed, "My daughter needs a job!" Can you imagine what is she saying to her own daughter?

For eighteen years, you attended classes, were involved in extracurricular activities, and perhaps secured a part-time job. This, plus socializing with your friends, was your job. Once you make your college choice and choose your classes, you once again default to attend classes, get involved in extracurricular activities, get a part-time job, and socialize with friends. This is what you know, so this is what you do.

The lack of job preparation and job search strategies during college is the reason why attaining a job right out of college is challenging and even discouraging. The problem may be in part that the college of your choice does a good job educating but may not provide enough direction for what is to come after college. It is best to start in your first year of college or as early as you can. A checklist of activities is presented in the beginning of each year in college to prepare for the transition to a career after college. It is a career planning process that you begin in the first year of college and complete in your last year of college.

THE CAREER PLANNING PROCESS

The advice given to students as they enter college is usually something like this:

Meet and interact with fellow students, advisors, and faculty. University life requires students to set priorities: attend class, write papers, take tests, read extensively, manage time, set academic goals, and at the same time satisfy family, work, and social obligations.

However, there is more to university life than what is stated here. The four years in college should prepare you for what happens once you graduate. In 2015, 1,855,000 students graduated with a bachelor's degree according to the National Association of Colleges and Employers (NACE). And, NACE states that it takes on the average seven months for new graduates to find employment. There is a lot of competition to get and keep a job in today's business environment.

Without a plan, a lot can happen. Students move back home, obtain a job unrelated to having a college degree, or fall into a depression. A feeling of hopelessness ensues. Feelings of being alone to figure next steps with parents wanting to know what your plans are for getting a job are unbearable. For most students, deciding on a career takes exploration.

Check It Off! offers you another way to approach college: *A career planning process to pursue while in college, so upon graduation the feeling of despair is replaced with hope.* The first two years of college is about obtaining a general education and deciding on a major. The third year is about choosing a major and deciding on a field of study. The final year is about the job search.

Meanwhile, networking, learning about different jobs and industries, understanding what jobs can use your talents, and obtaining the experience and skills are the approaches to securing a job you seek upon graduation.

Students in college incorporate many activities into their schedule while in college. Many students join clubs, play sports, attend concerts, participate in the arts, and listen to visiting lecturers. Students work part-time or full-time while attending college. Summer employment is more the norm than exception for most students.

There is no need to wait until after college to think about pursuing a career. Make choices in which activities you normally participate to support the career planning process. Take the opportunities that present themselves or you pursue during the four years of college to facilitate the process to obtain a job after college.

Real career satisfaction comes from being different and occupying a niche—differentiating yourself from others. The idea is to prepare and plan starting in the freshman year. Each year, you'll take on more activities and tasks to answer important career questions and prepare for life after college. This is the idea behind the checklist. Ultimately, in your final undergraduate year of college, you will be prepared for the transition from college to career.

Acknowledgments

It was May 2015 when I ventured out on a journey to write a book that meant a lot to me. Along the way, so many people offered support and feedback. I offer my deepest gratitude for your assistance in my endeavor.

First, thank you to my daughter, Stephanie Teller, who contributed her college experiences to add value and credibility to the concept of the book. And, to the many contributors as editors, my dearest friends, thank you: Anne-Marie Krause; Brenda Mendez; Michael Manahan; Maria Simpson, Ph.D.; Elaine Tamargo; Joyce Wedseltoft; and Cyndee Whitney, Ph.D.

Second, thank you to my class; the 2015 fall semester first-year students at California State University Dominguez Hills. Your input and suggestions contributed to the value of the book.

Third, thank you to my agent, Bertram Linder, for taking a chance on a first-time book author.

And finally, but more importantly, a huge thank you to a role-model and mentor who shared his knowledge and passion for writing, publishing, speaking, and teaching, Dr. Larry Rosen. Dr. Rosen lent his support and knowledge to an "unknown" author with the belief in the message

Thank you all from the bottom of my heart!

—*Vera Teller, Ph.D.*

Introduction

CHAPTER ORGANIZATION

What are the important tasks to complete throughout college in preparation for the job search? The answer, a *checklist* of activities you should complete each year while attending college to prepare for a career upon graduation. The idea behind the checklist is to pursue activities to facilitate the career planning process. The checklist is a "to do" list for career planning. It starts from having no or little idea on a college major and progresses to being prepared to enter the job market upon graduation.

The job search is not a passive activity. It is a proactive activity that should be treated like a project, with a project plan and schedule. This is the basis for the checklist. Ultimately, in the final undergraduate year of college, you will be prepared for the transition from college to career.

The checklist is organized by topic:
- Work Plan and Skill Assessment
- Academic Advising
- Career Support
- Academic Clubs and Professional Associations
- Portfolio
- Networking
- Experience and Employment

From the first year to the last year in college, various tasks are added to each topic for you to accomplish. Once the task is completed, you get to "Check It Off!" Refer to the Four Year Plan Checklist to review the topics and tasks to complete in order to prepare for the job search upon reaching graduation.

"Check It Off!" mentors you through the career planning process by offering advice on tasks to complete while in college in preparation to land a job just in time for graduation. Each task under the topic is clearly explained. Also, each chapter includes "don't waste time tips," notes, student stories relevant to points being made, and tools and techniques for the career planning process.

The job search is often thought of as an overwhelming task, but it is easier if you start as early as possible. The key to the job search is to stay positive, stay active, and be in control. In the "new career context," the individual is proactive rather than passive in career management. Self-confidence and competence are present. Waiting for the phone to ring or that all-important email to arrive places one in a passive position.

The job market is volatile and competitive. Use your time in college to prepare for the career you desire after college. *So, let's get started . . .*

Four Year Plan Checklist

Topic	First Year In College	Second Year In College	Third Year In College	Fourth Year In College
Work Plan and Skill Assessment	☐ Update the Work Plan ☐ Assess Oral and Written Communication Skills ☐ Assess Computer Skills	☐ Update the Work Plan ☐ Take a Writing Class	☐ Update the Work Plan ☐ Assess Job Skills in Related Field of Interest	☐ Update the Work Plan ☐ Make Use of the Internet ☐ Conduct a Self-Assessment
Academic Advising	☐ Obtain Academic Advising	☐ Obtain Academic Advising	☐ Obtain Academic Advising ☐ Explore Graduate School	☐ Obtain Academic Advising
Career Support	☐ Explore the Career Center ☐ Meet a Career Counselor ☐ Take Self-Assessment Tests ☐ Attend a Career Fair	☐ Meet with a Career Counselor ☐ Prepare an Elevator Speech ☐ Attend a Career Fair	☐ Meet with a Career Counselor ☐ Create a Personal Brand ☐ Realize the Importance of a Good Handshake ☐ Attend Career Fairs	☐ Meet With a Career Counselor ☐ Research the On-Campus Interview Program ☐ **Work** Career Fairs
Academic Clubs and Professional Associations	☐ Obtain a List of Campus Clubs ☐ Join at Least Two Clubs on Campus ☐ Research Professional Associations	☐ Run for Club Office ☐ Join Professional Associations	☐ Attain Leadership Role With Campus Clubs ☐ Attend Professional Association Meetings ☐ Join Toastmasters	☐ **Work** the Club Leadership Role ☐ **Work** Professional Association Meetings
Portfolio	☐ Review the Job Packet and Create an Aspirational Resume ☐ Obtain Letters of Recommendation ☐ Keep Outstanding Work ☐ Seek Award Opportunities	☐ Review Job Packet Information ☐ Continue to Obtain Letters of Recommendation, Keep Outstanding Work, Apply for Award Opportunities	☐ Prepare a Job Packet ☐ Continue to Obtain Letters of Recommendation, Keep Outstanding Work, Seek Awards and Scholarship Opportunities	☐ Update Portfolio ☐ Perfect Interviewing Skills
Networking	☐ Create a LinkedIn Account ☐ Attend at Least Two Networking Events ☐ Complete One Informational Interview	☐ Continue Using LinkedIn ☐ Attend at Least Two Networking Events ☐ Complete Two Informational Interviews	☐ Maintain Your LinkedIn Account ☐ Attend at Least Four Networking Events ☐ Complete Two Informational Interviews	☐ Use LinkedIn ☐ **Work** Networking Events ☐ Continue Informational Interviews
Experience and Employment	☐ Obtain Summer Employment, Part-Time Employment, or Volunteer in Career Field of Interest	☐ Interview Faculty in Career Field of Choice ☐ Shadow Career Professionals ☐ Research Employment Trends ☐ Obtain an Internship, Summer Employment, Part-Time Employment, or Volunteer in Career Field of Interest	☐ Research Companies of Interest ☐ Obtain an Internship, Summer Employment, Part-Time Employment, or Volunteer in Career Field of Interest	☐ Engage in the Job Search Campaign ☐ Obtain an Internship, Summer Employment, Part-Time Employment, or Volunteer in Career Field of Interest

Chapter One

Plan Before You Begin

"Would you tell me, please, which way I ought to go from here?"
"That depends a good deal on where you want to get to," said the Cat.
"I don't much care where—" said Alice.
"Then it doesn't matter which way you go," said the Cat.
"—so long as I get SOMEWHERE," Alice added as an explanation.
"Oh, you're sure to do that," said the Cat, "if you only walk long enough."

—Lewis Carroll, *Alice's Adventures in Wonderland*

Career planning and preparation is a process. During this process, much information is collected. Before you start, it is best to get organized.

CREATE PROFESSIONAL CONTACT ACCOUNTS

Creating professional contact accounts is an important step prior to seeking employment. As you enter college, it is best to create this once and be done with it.

First, create a professional e-mail address using your name or initials. You may want to keep this e-mail for just information related to your career. Your e-mail address should not be one used in high school or your college e-mail account.

Next, update your voice-mail greeting on a phone you plan to use for your job search. You want your voice message to sound professional, as if you are calling an office.

Finally, check your online presence. Remove photos that aren't "mom approved," for example. Employers do check social networking sites prior to an offer of employment. So, it is best to keep your online profile "mom approved" from the start.

Posted pictures and information on a social networking site can be used without your knowledge and in negative ways. Therefore, it is important that you carefully police your online presence, including what friends post about you or photos you are "tagged" in.

PREPARE A FILING SYSTEM

From the beginning of your college career to the day you retire, you will be creating and modifying a résumé, cover letters, and many other documents. You will see articles on interviewing, networking, or mentoring that you would like to keep for future reference. You will keep reference letters, important job documents, and so much more.

To start, keep your records electronically. Create a directory or document library and folders that you can reference easily. Also, remember to back up the document library regularly as you don't want to lose the information. It is as easy as saving the document library on a designated USB drive kept in your desk.

Your document library could include the following folders. The reason to number each folder, as this example illustrates, is to (a) keep the information in a particular order, and (b) plan for the chance of adding folders without disrupting the current configuration.

Career Planning
10. Work Plan
15. Résumé
20. Cover Letter
25. My Portfolio
30. Interview Information
35. Networking Information
40. Articles to Read
45. Internship Opportunities
50. Potential Employers
55. Associations
60. Events to Attend(ed)
65. Other Interesting Stuff

GENERATE A WORK PLAN

Next, generate a work plan. A work plan is the best and most efficient way to

a. assist with organization,
b. stay on schedule, and
c. set goals and review progress.

Assist with Organization

A work plan is a tracking system. It is an organized system to assist you in sticking to your career goals, organizing the job search, and listing tasks that must get done. A work plan is visual. It allows you to log the activities that are important to your college life, which will ultimately be valuable in your future job search. The work plan is the place where you will log those tasks that must be completed daily, weekly, or monthly.

Keeping track of what you need to do and what you have done keeps you organized and on track with career goals. Think of a work plan as an organized system to move you forward to accomplish your goals.

Stay on Schedule

Mapping out what you plan to do should help you stay on schedule. With a work plan, you will see that you cannot put off a task indefinitely. You will soon recognize that if a task can get done today, then you should do it today. Take Ben Franklin's good advice: "Don't put off until tomorrow what you can do today."

The work plan is a system for tracking the tasks that need to be done, as well as those that have been completed. It allows you to monitor your progress. It is the schedule to which you must hold yourself accountable.

Excel is one software tool to use for a work plan. With Excel, you can create separate worksheets for each college year and a worksheet for the job search. However, Excel is not the only planning or scheduling software. Use the Internet to download free software for planning and scheduling tasks or use whatever method you are comfortable with.

Set Goals and Review Progress

Setting up tasks, marking tasks completed, and achieving goals are the reasons for having a work plan. Reviewing the work plan on a continual basis and celebrating when completing milestones generate great feelings. Milestones are points within the work plan where you can celebrate success. Some examples are: completing a college course, joining a college club, completing a class presentation, or obtaining a job.

You can celebrate success in a number of ways, such as treating yourself to a special meal, buying a sought-after product, or opening a bottle of champagne. We all need to celebrate and have fun. The feelings that come when a goal is achieved are priceless!

Build the Work Plan

The work plan is the main document to log tasks you need to accomplish. First, open Excel (this is the suggested software method to use) and name your document Work Plan—version 1. Some people like to keep multiple versions of a document, while others like to update and modify one document. It is your choice. If you like to keep multiple versions of a document, then label the versions. You could add a version date as well. Save the Work Plan—version 1 to 10-Work Plan folder.

Rename the first worksheet in your document Work Plan—version 1, to *College Year 1*. Save the Work Plan document (Figure 1.1).

Next, label the columns as Task Number, Task, Start Date, End Date, Notes, and Status. The Task Number is a number given to each task to be completed. The number is written in increments of .05. This way, if you need to add a task it is easy to do so without disrupting the numbering sequence.

Next is the Task column. These are the tasks that you will need to work on in order to complete or meet your goals. Give each task a Start Date and End Date. These dates will help you measure your progress. Remember, the work plan is a planning tool, which may need to be updated periodically. If you don't meet these dates for a particular task, you can update the dates.

The last two columns are Notes and the Status of the task, whether it is completed, in progress, or not started. The Notes column is a place to record relevant information about the task as a visual reminder. Don't rely on your memory for noting anything that may be important. For example, if a contact person is out on vacation, remind yourself to call again in two weeks.

If a task is completed, shading the task row gray is sometimes helpful as a visual sign.

The logged tasks fall into topics. So, it is best to add headings to groups of tasks. This is helpful in identifying and visualizing the work plan process. The topics identified are shown in Table 1.1.

The work plan example in Figure 1.1 lists the topics. Your first step in the career planning process is to create this spreadsheet. You will begin to fill in the details in the subsequent chapters.

Task No.	Task	Start Date	End Date	Notes	Status
Work Plan and Skill Assessment					
1.05	Create Work Plan	5/15/2016	5/20/2016		In process
1.10	Assess oral skills	5/22/2016	9/26/2016	Taking a class in college, Year 2.	On hold
1.15	Assess writing skills	5/24/2016	5/24/2016		Postponed until after oral skills class
1.20	Assess computer skills	5/26/2016	5/26/2016	Need to learn more features on Excel. I will research classes in the area.	In process
Academic Advising					
2.05					
2.10					
2.15					
2.20					
Career Support					
3.05					
3.10					
3.15					
3.20					
Academic Clubs and Professional Associations					
4.05					
4.10					
4.15					
4.20					
Portfolio					
5.05					
5.10					
5.15					
5.20					
Networking					
6.05					
6.10					
6.15					
6.20					
Experience and Employment					
7.05					
7.10					
7.15					
7.20					

Figure 1.1. The Work Plan.

Table 1.1. The Work Plan Process

Topics	Definitions
Work plan and skill assessment	You will create a work plan for each year of college. Each year, you will evaluate the skills required for the career you want to pursue.
Academic advising	In the first two years of college, general academic advising is provided. Once a major is declared, academic advising becomes more specific.
Career support	Support is offered to students from various sources on campus. These sources are presented.
Academic clubs and professional associations	Research on academic clubs and professional associations affiliated with a career major is a process that is discussed throughout college.
Portfolio	The job packet needed for the job search is discussed throughout the four years.
Networking	A skill needed throughout your career is to network effectively. The definition of networking and effective networking techniques are presented.
Experience and employment	Prior to applying for permanent career positions, experience in the field of choice is essential. Ideas are offered on gaining this experience throughout college.

Chapter Two

First Year in College

"Who in the
World am I?
Ah, that's the great Puzzle!"

—Lewis Carroll, *Alice's Adventures in Wonderland*

The first year in college is an exploration of you, college, and career. Learn about yourself and gather information on all services available on campus. Start exploring majors of interest or your chosen career field. Meanwhile, explore career fields of interest by following your passion!

OVERVIEW

The freshman year is about self-exploration, which must come first, and then making decisions. Some students enter college with a specific major in mind, while other students enter college with the intent on changing majors. And some students just don't know their major interest. It could be that these students have many interests or are just uncertain. Regardless, if you are decided or undecided on a major, self-exploration is a step in the career planning process that cannot be skipped.

Don't be fooled by the term "self." You should *not* do self-exploration by yourself. So many students are hesitant about going through the self-awareness process with the help of a career counselor. It is to your benefit to seek help in the self-exploration process. Assessing your interests is the first step to the career planning process.

Before you decide on a career, take the time to complete the self-awareness and self-exploration process. Once you understand yourself—your likes,

7

First Year College Checklist

Work Plan and Skill Assessment	☐ Update the Work Plan ☐ Assess Oral and Written Communication Skills ☐ Assess Computer Skills
Academic Advising	☐ Obtain Academic Advising
Career Support	☐ Explore the Career Center ☐ Meet a Career Counselor ☐ Take Self-Assessment Tests ☐ Attend a Career Fair
Academic Clubs and Professional Associations	☐ Obtain a List of Campus Clubs ☐ Join at Least Two Clubs on Campus ☐ Research Professional Associations
Portfolio	☐ Review the Job Packet and Create an Aspirational Résumé ☐ Obtain Letters of Recommendation ☐ Keep Outstanding Work ☐ Seek Award Opportunities
Networking	☐ Create a LinkedIn Account ☐ Attend at Least Two Networking Events ☐ Complete One Informational Interview
Experience and Employment	☐ Obtain Summer or Part-Time Employment in a Career Field of Choice, or Volunteer in a Career Field of Choice

dislikes, passions, and motivations—you will be better prepared to go to the next step to pursue your career goals.

Advancing through college is a journey. Many students place focus and energy on the goal—graduation—but they don't enjoy the day-to-day activities of college. Engaging in the activities in the checklist will help you navigate through the chaos to a career choice.

Will you make mistakes? There are no mistakes—there are discoveries. On your journey, you are discovering what you like and want to pursue, as well as what you don't like and what you don't want to pursue. You will leave behind the "shoulds," such as "I should pursue technology because this is where all the high-paying jobs are going to be," to embrace the "wants." I want to learn more about marine biology. I really enjoy scuba diving and exploring marine life.

WORK PLAN AND SKILL ASSESSMENT

☐ Update the Work Plan

Add the tasks in the checklist to your Excel work plan under the first tab, College Year 1. Enter the task number, approximate start and end dates (during your freshman year), and notes for each task. The start and end dates are entered to monitor your progress in reaching your daily and weekly goals. Keep striving for these scheduled goals. The idea is to include these tasks into your schedule and aim to meet the dates.

☐ Assess Oral and Written Communication Skills

Oral and written communication skills rank high in terms of qualities sought by employers. The National Association of Colleges and Employers ranked the top ten candidate skills and qualities employers seek (*Job Outlook*, 2013):

1. Ability to verbally communicate with persons inside and outside the organization
2. Ability to work in a team structure
3. Ability to make decisions and solve problems
4. Ability to plan, organize, and prioritize work
5. Ability to obtain and process information
6. Ability to analyze quantitative data
7. Ability to grasp technical knowledge related to the job
8. Proficiency with computer software programs
9. Ability to create and edit written reports
10. Ability to sell or influence others

Communication skills mean reading, listening, nonverbal, speaking, and writing skills. Because e-mail is the communication forum most employees use in the workplace, the importance of written communication has significantly increased. In addition to e-mail, employees are often requested to write reports and media releases for various people, from executives to personnel at all levels of the organization (see Figure 2.1). Written materials are expected

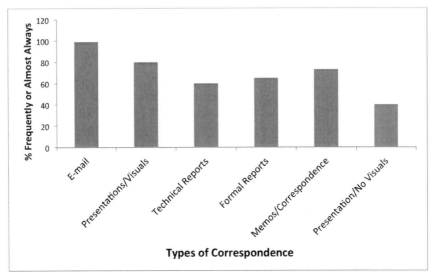

Figure 2.1. % Frequency of Various Forms of Writing in Most Companies. Report of the National Commission on Writing September 2004.

to be accurate, clear, and grammatically correct, regardless of the form of communication.

A 2004 report from the National Commission on Writing for America's families, schools, and colleges stated that writing is an essential skill for many. The commission surveyed 120 human resource directors. Sixty-four directors responded to the survey at a 53.3% response rate. The results of the survey indicated that two-thirds or more of their salaried employees had some responsibility for writing (see Figure 2.2). With the exception of mining and transportation/utilities, large majorities of salaried employees in all industries are expected to write as part of their job responsibilities.

The responding companies stated that they frequently or almost always take writing into consideration when hiring salaried employees. Writing samples are rarely required from job applicants. Applicants who submit résumés with grammatical or spelling errors and who provide poorly written application letters wouldn't get an interview, especially given the large pool of applicants who do present themselves well.

Communication skills must be learned. English grammar is taught in elementary school and continues through high school. However, college students still misuse the words "their," "there," and "they're." So, learning these "confusing words" is a must. College provides an opportunity to learn grammar and write well. If your courses do not teach grammar, or you have difficulty writing well, then you must seek help.

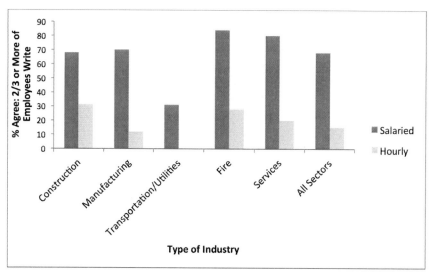

Figure 2.2. Most Professional Employees are Expected to Write. Report of the National Commission on Writing September 2004.

Many colleges have resources available through the various student services offered on campus. The Tutoring Center or Center for Learning and Academic Support Services or CLASS (Note: the name for the service can vary) is geared to help students learn the fundamental skills of grammar and mathematics. It is up to you to research the student services available on campus and seek help in the areas you are lacking or want to improve.

☐ **Assess Computer Skills**

Looking for a job has changed from the written form to the electronic form. The days of searching in the classified ads of a newspaper for a job are long gone. You are in a better position to look and apply for job postings if you are computer literate; knowing how to apply for jobs through the Internet is essential.

You must know how to use search engines like Google or Yahoo. Knowledge of MS Word is helpful in writing your résumé, cover letter, and references. Access to e-mail is critical. Many sites on the Internet offer free mailboxes; so check out Yahoo or Gmail to set up an e-mail account. Knowing how to manipulate social networking sites like LinkedIn is vital.

Assess whether or not you have the skills necessary to look for a job. If not, seek out courses to assist you to become familiar with a computer. Check your college classes first. Next, check the local library for a recommendation on local classes for computer education. Also, extension classes in cities, schools, or universities offer computer education classes at a reasonable price.

Funds are available to cover costs of retraining or additional career training, if required. Check with your local library to find the funds available for these programs.

ACADEMIC ADVISING

☐ Obtain Academic Advising

The new college student knows very little about college and the college system (how it works and functions). The first-year student should ask questions! However, this is a paradox. The first year student doesn't know what questions to ask. A visit to the Academic Advising Office or Undergraduate Advisement Center on campus is a good place to start learning about college.

The Academic Advising Office has advisors for students called academic advisors who counsel students on which courses to take each semester and each year.

Students are urged to meet with an advisor each semester before registration to ensure that concentration and graduation requirements are met. Usually, the ratio of student to advisor can range from twenty to hundreds to a single advisor. Therefore, it is the responsibility of students to know who their academic advisor is and visit this person regularly.

Students should contact the Academic Advisement Office with general questions. You will receive detailed information regarding classes, selection of major, graduation requirements, transfer of credit, and special circumstances and conditions. Academic advising should be used for help in selecting courses, understanding academic regulations, and gaining perspective on academic programming. Often, an appointment is required. So, don't wait to schedule an appointment. Add this task to your work plan.

Note the information shared by Dr. Cuseo below:

> Meetings need to take place at times when advisors have sufficient time to interact with students as persons—rather than "process" them as registrants, and when advisors have the opportunity to explore or clarify students' broader, long-term educational plans—rather than focusing narrowly, myopically, and episodically on the imminent, deadline-driven task of class scheduling (Cuseo, 2005).

The academic advisor has information for freshmen about academic resources, general education courses and descriptions, change of majors, and academic probation and disqualification. Talk to the academic advisor about taking general studies courses that will provide you with the opportunity to explore career fields of interest. If undecided and confused regarding selecting a career field, the best option is to take various courses of interest to begin to narrow your search.

CAREER SUPPORT

☐ **Explore the Career Center**

Most, if not all, college campuses have a Career Center. Most third- or fourth-year students do not visit the Career Center even once while on campus. This is unfortunate since students pay for the Career Center services with their tuition money and the Career Center has much to offer students.

Take advantage of the offerings of the Career Center. It provides career counseling and career and employment services, which include, but are not limited to, job fairs, job listing database, individual career counseling, and assessment tests. The Career Center provides assistance with on-campus interviews; workshops on career topics; and support with résumés, cover letters, interview skills, and the job search. The Career Center is there to assist you in your career planning.

You don't need to have settled on a career to visit the Career Center. The Career Center can help with unanswered questions. The three most important questions for new college students are:

1. What do I like to do?
2. What do I want to do?
3. What does the world need?

A career will occupy a majority of time in your life; so you want to pursue a field that you enjoy. The first step in the career journey is to get to know you. Most of the time, we learn about ourselves—our morals, values, attitudes, interests, and passions—when confronted with a problem. How do we handle ourselves? Do we shy away or attack the problem? Do we seek help or try to go it alone? There are no "right" or "wrong" answers. It is a personality type that we have to get to know and embrace.

If you don't like certain characteristics about yourself, then you can work to change. But first, self-awareness—getting to know you—is the fundamental task for the freshman year. As you begin to know your preferences, you can begin to make good decisions for your career and life.

The first task is to find the Career Center and ask for a tour. Obtain all of the career manuals and brochures published by the Career Center. Find out what is available online. What are the website URLs? Also, find out about the employee structure at the Career Center. Who are the directors, managers, counselors, and the like? Is there an organizational chart? The organizational chart provides the big picture of the services available to students.

For example, if there are no career counselors on staff, then they may not offer this service. Or, this service may be outsourced to another company. If the college does have career counselors on staff, then what are their areas of specialization? Just in case you need a special service in the future, it is best to obtain this information now.

☐ Meet a Career Counselor

Choosing a major can be a confusing process. The good news is that the Career Center can help! A career counselor offers information and services to assist you in making wise decisions. The counselors can offer suggestions, provide access to assessment tests, and make recommendations. They can help you analyze your assessment test results and assist you to focus on short-term and then long-term goals. Make an appointment with several career counselors and choose someone you like. You should feel comfortable with this person and not intimidated.

(Note: Some universities don't give a choice of counselors as they are assigned based on the college within the university and year. A suggestion is to check the university's website and drop-in to visit.)

☐ Take Self-Assessment Tests

Self-assessment is the process of gathering information about yourself in order to make informed career decisions. Self-assessment tests are the tools to find out that information. Assessment tests or career aptitude tests are geared to reveal your values, abilities or skills, interests, and personality type. Once you assess information about yourself, you then can relate it to majors and career choices. Assessment and aptitude tests provide a framework for you in making career choices. A "picture" of your abilities and skills is mapped with interests to find career choices.

This is the first step in career planning, which is often overlooked. When students hear the word "test," they may assume that there is a right answer. Assessments do not have right and wrong answers. They highlight individual characteristics about you. Learning about yourself first, and then mapping your individual characteristics to a career that suits your personality and abilities, is the strategy to lead a fulfilling and satisfying life. Now that this is explained, you can understand the value of not skipping this step in the career planning process and answering the questions honestly!

The Myers-Briggs Type Indicator®

One assessment and widely known indicator used by many organizations is the Myers-Briggs Type Indicator (MBTI®). The purpose of the MBTI personality inventory is to make the theory of psychological types described by C. G. Jung understandable and useful in people's lives. This assessment, or one similar, is offered by colleges. The MBTI outlines four dimensions of psychological type:

- Extrovert/Introvert: This dimension signifies whether you draw energy from other people (extrovert) or from yourself (introvert).
- Sensation/Intuition: This dimension determines your preference in gathering and processing information. Sensing-type people describe themselves as practical. Intuitive-type people describe themselves as innovative and conceptual.
- Thinking/Feeling: If you are rated as a Thinking person, your judgment is objective and logical. If you are rated as a Feeling person, your judgment is subjective and personal.
- Judgment/Perception: The fourth dimension describes a person's attitude regarding structure. Judgment-type people like closure and task completion. Perceiving types prefer to keep things open and flexible.

The Strong Interest Inventory

The Strong Interest Inventory assessment measures career and leisure interests. It is based on the work of E. K. Strong, Jr., who originally published his inventory on the measurement of interests in 1927. In 1974, John Holland's psychology-based codes were incorporated into the assessment. The six categories are Realistic, Investigative, Artistic, Social, Enterprising, and Conventional. The Strong Interest Inventory assessment is used for the following reasons:

- College major choice, to help students identify areas of interest and link to a particular college major
- Career exploration, to help students identify areas of interest and link to various occupations and careers
- Career development, to provide a heightened self-awareness to students by recognizing individual strengths in areas that are overlooked or not recognized, including a work style and risk-taking orientation

Focus 2

Focus 2 combines self-assessment, career and major exploration, decision making, and action planning in one product and is often available on college campuses. Focus 2 guides students through a career and education decision-making model to help them select their majors and make informed career decisions.

Appendix A lists Internet sites accessed for free where you can take a modified version of the aptitude and assessment tests listed earlier.

☐ Attend a Career Fair

What is a career fair or job fair? The college, usually the Career Center, organizes a career fair once or twice a year. The Career Center organizes representatives from businesses to talk and interview students for potential jobs. A career fair is an opportunity for students to meet with employers they may not be able to access any other way. The idea behind attending career fairs in years one and two is to get used to the process before you need it!

There are conflicting opinions regarding career fairs. Some people do not like to compete with the crowds attending the job fairs. Because there are so many people, it is difficult to talk "seriously" to a company representative. Other individuals like job fairs. This is an opportunity to meet employees from various organizations with which you may or may not be familiar.

As a freshman in college, your task is to attend a job fair. If the job fair has workshops or seminars, attend them. Walk around the job fair and observe and notice what other students are doing. Take notes. It is difficult to remember the many employers at the job fair. You might take down the name of the organization that has the longest line and then do some online research about the company, at a later date.

Finally, NETWORK! Talk to other students. Ask questions. Do they have a copy of their résumé with them? What questions are they going to ask the representative? Be inquisitive and show initiative. Demonstrate your interest in learning what the students are trying to accomplish. You do this because, in subsequent years, you will be attending a career fair for important reasons. For now, consider your attendance a learning experience.

ACADEMIC CLUBS AND PROFESSIONAL ASSOCIATIONS

☐ Obtain a List of Campus Clubs

College is the time of exploration through joining athletic programs, fraternities, sororities, and clubs. There are so many choices. Usually, the list of clubs is posted on the university website. If this is not available, contact the Student Center. If there is a day at the college to showcase all of the clubs, then take the time to view the clubs that are available on campus. Talk to the people running the clubs, obtain the information on the clubs of interest, and attend one or two meetings.

☐ Join at Least Two Clubs on Campus

When college students think about joining a fraternity, sorority, or club, they think FUN! However, this is an area where you need to think "career planning." For example, if you are interested in pursuing a career in accounting, then you should join the Accounting Club. This accomplishes three things.

First, you meet other students in your field of interest. You must always think of "networking" when in college.

Second, this will confirm or refute your interest in the field. If you find you don't like the students or have little in common with these students, then this might not be your field of choice. If you find a group of students "just like me," then you have found your niche.

Third, you will add participation in the Accounting Club to your résumé. Once again, this is one way to differentiate you from other job candidates. If you are seeking a career in accounting and have participated in an Accounting Club for several years, then this illustrates to a prospective employer your passion and interest in the accounting profession. You will get even more credit from a prospective employer if you have served as a member of the club's executive committee.

It is recommended that you choose at least two clubs to join in your freshman year in college. The reason (if it isn't obvious by now) is self-exploration. This is the time of discovery. If you always had a passion for acting, but never thought you could possibly pursue this field as a career, why not join the Acting Club? This is a very easy way to pursue a dream with very little investment. If it works out, then you'll have to reassess your career strategy. What does "if it works out" mean? It means, are you looking forward to going to the club? Do you enjoy the people? Is this a field that you enjoy learning about? Then you have found your niche. If it doesn't work out, then you'll know. Cross that idea off the list!

☐ Research Professional Associations

Take the idea of campus clubs and now apply it to the real world—they're called professional associations. These associations exist for almost every job classification and/or profession possible. Usually, there is a cost to join the association, but students are offered a discounted rate. New and young members sustain the association; so college students are sought after and encouraged to participate.

Appendix B lists (some) associations by career field. However, the key is to research before joining the association. Contact the professors in your area of interest and ask what associations are particularly noteworthy. Use the Internet to determine the goals and objectives of the association. If your interests are in alignment with the association's goals and objectives, pursue joining. Find a branch of the association that is local. If you present yourself as a college student who is researching the association to join, most associations will allow you to attend a couple of sessions for free.

The reasons for joining an association are as important, if not more so, than joining a college club: networking, finding your niche, and adding the association's name to your résumé. There are additional benefits to joining an association. (Although this sounds redundant, it is very important.) While the additional benefits to joining an association are not significant at this point in your college career, the main thing is to verify that the field you are pursuing is the career field of choice.

If not, then now is the time to move on and explore another choice. Many students drop out of college stating, "I don't know what I want to do." Dropping out of college is not the answer. The answer doesn't just "come" to you; the answer is in the exploration. So, get out there and explore. Find your community. You will know when you find the group of people with whom you feel connected to and a passion to be with.

PORTFOLIO

In your first year of college, begin compiling information that you will take on interviews, as you never go into an interview empty handed. This collection of information is called a portfolio. A portfolio is a great way to show off your best work to a potential employer. Obtain a three-ring binder and create the following sections: job packet, letters of recommendation, work examples, and award certificates. During your time in college, you will be adding documents to the various sections of the binder. Table 2.1 gives a description of the work included in the portfolio.

☐ Review the Job Packet and Create an Aspirational Résumé

When you begin to interview for job positions you will need a résumé, cover letter, stellar references, and business cards. The résumé and cover letter are written for a specific job advertisement found on the Internet, and the like. This information will be discussed in detail in the next chapter(s).

Table 2.1. The Portfolio

Portfolio Item	Description
Job packet	This includes job advertisement, résumé (or Aspirational Résumé for the first year in college), cover letter, stellar references, and business cards. The job packet information is discussed in the next chapter.
Letters of recommendation	These letters are written about you from previous employers (includes volunteer work), usually your boss, teachers, coaches, or anyone in a management level who reviews your work.
Examples of your work	Any work you created for an organization, whether for profit, nonprofit, or school, and that shows your potential, shows future employers that you have promise. (Be careful as work you have produced for an employer may be covered by confidentiality and/or copyright protection.)
Award certificates	Copies of award certificates obtained after high school. (High school doesn't count anymore.)

For the first year in college, you might consider completing an Aspirational Résumé. The Aspirational Résumé, located in Appendix C, is a tool used to focus on the college years. The sections of the Aspirational Résumé include Objective, Education, Relevant Experience, Memberships and Clubs, and Personal Notes/Ideas. Once again, just like the Work Plan introduced in Chapter One, the Aspirational Résumé is a planning tool. Beginning to think about a long-term plan of what you would like to achieve over the next four years is the basis for the exercise.

Completing an Aspirational Résumé is an iterative process. Start by filling out the sections that you know. Then, take a break and work on the résumé again. Look at the list of campus clubs and professional associations, decide on which ones you would like to pursue, and add that information to the Aspirational Résumé. Continue with the same format: research, make decisions, and include in the Aspirational Résumé. Things that are important now might not be important later, and that is okay. An Aspirational Résumé changes over time, and provides a "big picture" on what you would like to accomplish or "aspire to" doing and completing during your college years.

☐ **Obtain Letters of Recommendation**

Start now to collect letters of recommendation. As you are taking classes and receive an excellent grade, reach out to that professor to write a letter of recommendation. If you play a sport in college, ask your coach for a letter of recommendation. A professor, teacher, coach, or former employer reinforcing your ability by writing a letter of recommendation is impressive to a potential employer. Showcasing your various professional relationships is a great way for a potential employer to get to know you, your talents, and your skills.

If you are interested in graduate school, awards, or scholarship applications, letters of recommendation are often required. So, collecting these letters as you navigate through college is easier than "hunting" down professors in the future. *Many professors are adjunct or temporary and difficult to locate once the semester is completed.*

Let's not get confused. *Letters of recommendation and "job references" are two different things.* Job references are a bigger deal, and we'll talk about that in future chapters. But for right now, after you are interviewed, if an employer is seriously considering hiring you, you will be asked for job references. These are names and contact information from people willing to speak on your behalf. I call these people your "stellar references." These are people who know you very well. Generally, you should have three to five people who are stellar references. As you progress in your career, this list should grow to six or more.

Letters of recommendation should be collected when you finish a course, internship, job, or volunteer position. If you think you did a good job, then ask for a letter of recommendation. You should keep in touch with the people you have worked with after you leave college, a course, job, and the like. But there is a time when that doesn't happen. So, the next best thing is a letter of recommendation to add to your portfolio.

Asking someone to write a letter of recommendation is a simple task. You simply state, "My position at this company is coming to an end in two weeks. My reviews are good, and my professionalism on the job is good. I've met all the department deadlines and procedures over the two years I've been employed. Could I ask you to write a letter of recommendation for me? I would really appreciate it. I would like to have the letter prior to my last day on the job. Thank you." (Note that some people don't want to write letters of recommendation because they are too busy. In that case, offer to write the letter for them, and all they have to do is sign it.)

☐ Keep Outstanding Work

Any great written paper, project, or presentation that was given during school should be kept in your portfolio. Keep all spectacular examples of your work to present when on an interview.

During a college course, when an assignment is given, think of this assignment as an opportunity to showcase your potential to an employer. Most students write papers, participate in a team project, or prepare a presentation to fulfill course requirements. Why not use this opportunity to think visionary? Can I use this opportunity to showcase my writing skills, organizational skills, or leadership skills to a prospective employer? Now, the perspective of completing this assignment has changed from "getting a grade" to showcase the completed assignment to a perspective employer during an interview.

SMART IDEA:

DON'T WASTE TIME

During college, whenever possible, if given the option to select a topic or presentation, choose a topic that is career related. For example: What are the top companies to work for and why? If interested in history, what are some careers associated with this major? What is the skill set employers are looking for once you graduate with a "marketing" degree?

☐ Seek Award Opportunities

A secret on many college campuses are the numerous scholarships available to students. Most scholarships have specific criteria. For example, a scholarship is given to a student who is enrolled in a specific major and living in a specific zip code—nothing to do with financial need. Some scholarships are for financial-need students. You need to read the information on the specific scholarship to know the requirements.

The effort required to apply for a scholarship is minimal compared to the reward. Usually, a one-page written statement on the reasons you should receive the scholarship and a transcript record are required. The payoff is not only monetary but also an entry on your résumé. These "small" but significant awards distinguish you from every other student applying for a job after college. Contact your academic advisor or check the university's website to find out when the scholarship award list is posted, so that you can read the criteria and apply for the scholarships before the deadline. Once again, this is another task to add to your work plan.

NETWORKING

Networking is beneficial and will take on increasing importance in decades to come because of the changing nature of the work environment. Glass and Brody (2006), in their book *You Can't Do It Alone*, defined "networking" as sharing information and resources. Keith Ferrazzi, in his 2005 bestseller

Never Eat Alone, described networking as "connecting—sharing my knowledge and resources, time and energy, friends and associates, and empathy and compassion in a continual effort to provide value to others, while coincidentally increasing my own." A presentation given by Leah Moran Rampy, PhD, in 2009, "Build Your Network and Get It Working for You," described networking as

Building and sustaining a web of relationships that enables us to:

- support others by introducing them to individuals who can offer suggestions, advice, or introductions, and
- receive suggestions, advice, or introductions from others in support of professional goals.

People are networking within all areas of their lives, not just for career advancement or job employment. But, there is confusion as to the difference between networking for career and job-related issues and social networking in general.

Here is the one most important fact you need to know about networking. *Networking is credited as being the most successful means to finding employment.* The U.S. Department of Labor (2014) *reported* that most jobs are obtained through networking. Although the statistic changes every year, on average, 50% of the way people obtain jobs is through networking. Some statistics go as high as 80%. Regardless of the statistic, networking becomes more important as you obtain more experience in your chosen field of work.

Some people think that networking is about

- going to networking events and furiously exchanging business cards,
- schmoozing as a superficial way of meeting people, or
- giving a lot to others, while getting little.

Most people hate the idea of networking, don't think they have the time to network, or just don't think the results are worth the effort. Networking works. A network can provide emotional support when needed, help you achieve your goals, provide opportunities to learn more about your field, and assist you in seeking new job opportunities.

Many authors have proposed unique definitions for the term "networking" and instruction on how to increase one's network. Still, there is a lack of clarity on the meaning of the term. This lack of clarity can lead to confusion and misperception as to the needs of parties within the networking relationship and the potential outcomes of the relationship.

Also, attending conferences and exchanging business cards, or attending events after work to build relationships are touted by many authors as the way to build your network. Authors of networking books stress taking time to devote to networking and staying connected. Make the networking task work for you.

Networking is about strategizing—using your time effectively to cultivate those relationships that help you fulfill both career goals and provide the support you need for career decisions.

Origins of Networking

The origin of networking is patterned after the mentor–protégé relationship, familiar, yet misunderstood by many. Even today, researchers do not agree on the definition of a "mentor" or "protégé" or the characteristics of the relationship. Because individuals historically stayed within an organization for thirty or more years, having a mentor was credited and highly documented as the means to advance in one's career. More than a decade or more ago, working for a single organization over the course of one's career was considered normal. Employers were hesitant to hire those who changed organizations frequently as those habits were considered flighty. That has changed!

The mentor–protégé relationship was developed in response to the hierarchical structure of the organization during the Industrial Age, to help others advance up the career ladder within an organization. The literature shows clearly that the mentor relationship is hierarchical; the mentor is in a higher position than the protégé. While this higher position worked for men, it worked less well for women. The predominance of men in the corporation, during this period, added to the difficulties women had in establishing cross-gender mentor relationships and the inaccessibility women have had to other women in executive positions.

"Mentoring" was seen as the most important technique or tool contributing to advancement within the corporation. Those who were mentored reported a higher rate of promotion compared with those who were not mentored. Interestingly, those who were mentored also reported higher levels of career satisfaction and compensation than those who were not mentored.

Some organizations recognized the value of mentor relationships and tried to formalize them, as part of the planned career development of women, minorities, junior managers, and other professionals. These programs have three primary goals:

1. To assist women and minorities, those who do not have access to senior white males within the organization to foster their development;
2. To provide the less experienced person with a more experienced person, in order to foster the development of both; and

3. To retain new employees, develop their skills, and help them to adapt to the organizational culture.

These programs are still prominent in organizations today. However, times have changed. Although many of us would love to stay in an organization long enough to derive the benefits of a mentor relationship, it just doesn't happen like this anymore. The changes in the work environment, due to globalization and information technology, forced a shift in viewing the traditional one-on-one mentor–protégé relationship as the optimum relationship credited for an individual's career advancement and support. The "new" career context of mentoring states that individuals draw career opportunities and support from a myriad of relationships described as networks. These relationships can include mentors but also include superiors, peers, subordinates, friends, and family (see Figure 2.3).

By studying the benefits of the traditional relationship of a mentor to the protégé as a supportive relationship to aid in career advancement and provide emotional support, the new perspective on the mentor relationship termed "networks" is expanded to include all individuals responsible for career advancement and emotional support. The new mentoring literature highlights the importance of all relationships for continued growth and development in adulthood. The benefits reserved for the chosen protégé within the traditional one-on-one mentor relationship are now expanded to include a multi-relational network, providing the individual with unlimited potential for opportunities.

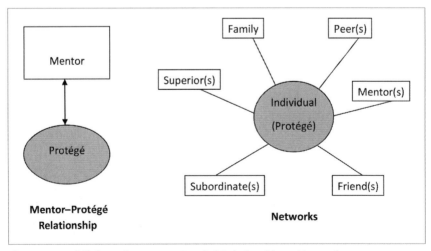

Figure 2.3.   Shift from the Mentor–Protégé Relationship to Networks.

Networking Defined

Research substantiates the theory of networks. Kathy Kram's (1988) seminal work, *Mentoring at Work: Developmental Relationships in Organizational Life*, defined a network as the set of relationships an individual has with people who take an active interest in, and action to advance, the individual's career by assisting with his or her personal and professional development. The definition of networking has been widened to include personal development.

Work by seminal researchers in the field of mentoring documented the distinct functions of the mentor relationship. This was done for various reasons.

One reason was to duplicate the relationship for women and minorities, groups deemed suppressed by the corporate structure. Another reason was to study the various types of relationships to make networking productive.

The work by researchers split the functions derived by the relationship into two groups: career functions and emotional support. *Career functions* may include providing sponsorship, exposure and visibility, coaching, protection, and challenging assignments. *Emotional support* is directed toward enhancing one's sense of competence, clarity of identity, and sense of self. These functions also include role modeling, acceptance and confirmation, counseling, and friendship.

By organizing our relationships as providing high or low levels of career advancement or emotional needs, the following classifications were developed. A *mentor* is a person who provides both a high amount of career functions and emotional support. A *sponsor* provides a high amount of career functions but offers little emotional support. Of course, a *friend* would provide little toward career functions but a high amount of emotional support. Lastly, an *ally* provides little toward career functions and emotional support (Higgins, 2000) (see Table 2.2).

Networking is about strategizing—using your time effectively to cultivate those relationships that help fulfill both career goals and also provide emotional support. Networking is about identifying those people who can offer the support you need to help you achieve your goals.

Table 2.2. Types of Networking Relationships

Relationship	Career Functions	Emotional Support
Mentor	High amount	High amount
Sponsor	High amount	Low amount
Friend	Low amount	High amount
Ally	Low amount	Low amount

Types of Networks

What types of networking relationships are best when seeking career advancement? What types of networking relationships are best when looking for employment? Networks are divided into two sections: internal networks and external networks. Examples of people within your *internal network* are:

- Relatives
- Friends
- Friends of relatives
- Spouse's relatives
- College alumni
- Professional and social organizations
- Parents of your children's friends
- Neighbors, past, and present
- People you went to school with
- Work colleagues
- People in your religious congregation
- Former teachers and employers
- People you socialize with
- People who provide services to you (doctor, lawyer, accountant, etc.)
- People you meet when you volunteer: clubs, associations, and the like.
- Recruiters

External networks are people you meet when engaging in networking activities such as:

- Recruiters in your field of business
- Completing informational interviews
- Attending career fairs
- Attending networking events
- Taking a class
- Working in an organization

Our first jobs are usually obtained through people we know: our internal network (Teller, 2008). In subsequent chapters, the benefits derived from the different types of networking contacts will be explained.

☐ **Create a LinkedIn Account**

LinkedIn is a *social networking* site. It was designed specifically for the business community, but people from all different fields use the site. The goal of the site is to allow registered members to establish and document networks of people they know and trust professionally.

What Is Social Networking?

A social network service focuses on building online communities of people who share common interests and activities. Most social network services provide a wide variety of ways for users to interact, such as e-mail message boards and instant messaging services. Social networks connect people at low cost; this can be beneficial for anybody looking to expand his or her contact base or keep in touch with existing contacts.

Social Networking in Business

LinkedIn.com is a popular social network that aims to interconnect professionals. It claims to have more than 30 million registered users from 150 different industries (this number changes regularly). LinkedIn is used by job-seekers. It can link users with past colleagues, and you have the opportunity to link to certain companies you aspire to work for.

Once you have created a LinkedIn account, you have the ability to do the following:

- Create a professional profile
- Develop a network of connections
- Search for jobs
- Search for people
- Send messages to your connections (there might be a cost associated with "the number of messages")
- Receive requests for introductions
- Participate in LinkedIn Groups
- Participate in LinkedIn Answers

To get started, go to: www.LinkedIn.com. What you will need is a user name and valid e-mail address.

With any software on the market, companies update the software regularly. It is best to log on and do your best to navigate the site on your own. However, with most software there are basics. With LinkedIn one of the basics to the application is creating a profile. It is important to note that your résumé and LinkedIn profile must be in sync. Employers review both.

Navigating LinkedIn

There are several links on the top navigation menu. (Again, these links change.) The major links are Home–return to the LinkedIn home page;

Profile—edit or view your profile and recommendations; Contacts—manage, add, and import connections; Groups—view your groups, view a group directory, or create a group; Jobs—perform an advanced job search or manage job postings; and Inbox—view, send, and archive LinkedIn messages.

Your task in the freshman year is to create a LinkedIn account and profile. Add as many internal network contacts as you can. In the long term, as you start to attend networking events, you will add external contacts to your LinkedIn account.

As a first-year student, learn how to navigate the system, so that you become comfortable with the software. Then, create a basic profile, add connections, and join groups of interest.

Create a Basic Profile

1. *Customize your LinkedIn URL.* Use a professional URL address, using your name, as you will have this address for a long time. This makes it easier for people to find you by searching for your name. You may want to check how many people are registered on the site with your name. After you have done that, you can determine what your URL address will be. The idea is to choose a name that those who know you will recognize. Editing your URL is usually done by choosing "Edit Profile." LinkedIn updates the site frequently; so directions on how to change the URL may not remain current or up-to-date.

2. *Profile content.* Make your profile content substantial and interesting. Don't be afraid to show your personality but always maintain professionalism. Keep your profile updated with the most current information.

3. *Profile picture.* Your photograph is a visual representation of who you are to the world of LinkedIn. Make a great first impression with a professional-looking photograph. The best are high-quality head shots with simple backgrounds. Make sure you come across as personable and friendly in the head shot. A photograph of you with a smile is usually best. Your personal style, from your hair to your clothing and for women makeup, communicates a lot about you. Unfortunately, we are judged on the way we look. If you don't believe me, look into the sales of all of the women's magazines such as *Vogue*.

4. *Summary.* The summary is the focal point of the LinkedIn profile. This is the area within LinkedIn to showcase your skill set. This is the space to differentiate you from all the other professionals in your industry or job market.

5. *Education.* List all schools you are attending or have attended (excluding high school) along with their website and a direct link. This is a good place to put any education certifications or special technical training that you received or are working toward.

Make Connections

Connect to people with whom you have a direct connection, your internal network people, and the people you know. If you find contacts who are already LinkedIn members, you can add them to your network by sending them a request.

Add Groups

LinkedIn Groups allows you to meet and interact with others who have similar interests. You can search the group directory for your particular industry, geographic location, or even hobby interests. Most likely, your college or university will have a LinkedIn group. Join that group first.

Groups will post ongoing discussions to which you can add your comments or share your expertise. Once again, search for industry groups related to the career you want to pursue. If you find that you enjoy reading the information that is shared from that group, then you are in the right career. If not, this is the time to recognize that this career is not for you. You can add groups in areas you have an interest or passion but are hesitant to pursue as a career. This is another way to explore career options without too much of an investment.

☐ Attend at Least Two Networking Events

It is important to become comfortable attending networking events. In the freshman year of college, your task is to find two events to attend. This could include the clubs or professional associations you are considering joining. Your assignment is to make small talk with the people you meet, ask questions, and listen.

It is best to attend networking events alone. Most often, students travel in packs. These students don't venture out alone unless it is to go home or to meet mom and dad for dinner. You have to start being comfortable attending events alone. This serves a couple of purposes. First, if you attend a function with another person, you will probably stay with that person the entire evening and not feel comfortable enough to venture out and meet other people. Second, the intent of attending networking events is to meet people you don't know.

Set a small goal for yourself at a networking event. A small goal could be as simple as collecting four business cards from people you do not know. Engage in polite conversation by introducing yourself and asking the person a question or two. Why are they attending the event? Have they been a member of the organization for a long time?

Since you are a new member or considering becoming a new member, ask individuals what they can tell you about the organization that you should know. At the end of the conversation, ask the individual for his or her business card. If you have a business card, offer one of yours. Write a few descriptive sentences about the person you met on your business card, so that you will remember the person the next day. Of course, find that person on LinkedIn the following day and add to your contact database.

☐ Complete One Informational Interview

An "informational interview" is not a "job interview." An informational interview is an opportunity to collect information from the interviewee regarding their area of expertise or career path. When requesting an "informational interview," you must use this term; do not say "request for an interview." That will send the wrong message to the person you want to meet regarding his or her career path.

You want to meet someone in your field of interest to discuss the career field. How do you meet someone in your field of interest? One way of doing this is to find someone in the organization, if you work part-time, who works in your field of interest. Contact at least one person who works in your field of interest and invite that person out for coffee or lunch.

A sample e-mail to request an informational interview might look like this:

To: Mr. Smith
From: Jane Templeton
Subject: Informational Interview Request

Dear Mr. Smith,

I am a student at California State University, Dominguez Hills studying accounting. I will be graduating in a year, and my accounting professor, Dr. Dobson, stated it would be beneficial to talk with someone in my field of interest.

I'm interested in your career advancement and would like to discuss the CPA test, too.

I'll be in your area next week and would like to meet for coffee or lunch to discuss your career. Please let me know if you will be available, as I look forward to talking with you.

Sincerely,
Jane Templeton
JaneTempleton@xxx.com
Mobile: 999-999-9999

Just like a "regular job interview," a certain protocol must be followed when asking for an "informational interview."

- Do not ask for a job. This is an informational interview, not a job interview.
- Be prepared to talk with this person. Have your questions ready. You must be knowledgeable about the company.
- Be respectful of time. When asking a person for coffee or lunch, ask how much time he or she can spend talking with you and respect that time frame.
- Follow up after the conversation with a "thank you" e-mail. Be courteous and respectful.

Ask the person about his or her day-to-day activities. Ask questions regarding the job. What are some of the activities the person enjoys? What are some of the activities the person doesn't care for but must do? Ask about industry trends, business culture, and opportunities. Don't forget to ask for a business card and add that person to your LinkedIn network. It is less formidable after you complete this exercise once.

EXPERIENCE AND EMPLOYMENT

☐ **Obtain Summer or Part-Time Employment in the Career Field of Choice, or Volunteer in the Career Field of Choice**

One question most interviewers ask on an interview is, "Do you have any experience in this field?" And, your reply is, "I've just spent four years in college educating myself in this field." The reply from the prospective employer is then, "Yes, but do you have any experience in this field?"

You need experience in your chosen field of study before you seek employment in your career field. There are several ways to go about getting experience:

1. Seek part-time employment in an area of interest. If you are interested in law, find a part-time position in a law office. This can work for a variety of businesses, such as accounting, medicine, finance, sports, and entertainment. Even if you are not working in that field, being exposed to the environment is the next best thing.
2. Seek part-time employment in a nonprofit organization specific to your area of interest. If you are interested in pursuing marketing, then offer to create marketing materials for the organization.
3. Volunteer to work at a nonprofit organization for a short period of time to learn the business and foster contacts. Nonprofit organizations provide an excellent opportunity for individuals lacking experience. Nonprofit organizations thrive on volunteerism. These organizations do a lot of good work with very little overhead and need volunteers to assist in doing a lot of work. Contact the executive director of a nonprofit organization and offer to work in your field of choice as an assistant.

The purpose of working is to gain skills and qualifications for the position that you are interested in pursuing and to be exposed to the environment. It is vital for you to be exposed to and learn the industry lingo, acronyms, and jargon. By being around the office or profession, you will pick up this information. You should be aware of the key people in the industry and region. It is important to know who runs the organization and the organizational chart. Also, pay attention to changes in the industry. Be aware of companies within the industry that went out of business, mergers with other companies, new products introduced, or major issues within the business.

Once again, this is an excellent opportunity to network with people working in your field of interest. Take advantage of this opportunity by completing an informational interview or asking people out for coffee or lunch. You will learn a lot. You will learn if you enjoy this selected field and its people. You will learn if you "fit in." You will learn if this is the industry that gives you the drive and motivation to get up from bed and go to work every day.

The first year is a year of exploration and discovery about you and your passions. The best way to find out about you is to get up, get out, and get involved!

 **Check It Off!**

Review the first year in college checklist. How many activities are you able to check off?

☐ Update the Work Plan
☐ Assess Oral and Written Communication Skills
☐ Assess Computer Skills
☐ Obtain Academic Advising
☐ Explore the Career Center
☐ Meet a Career Counselor
☐ Take Self-Assessment Tests
☐ Attend a Career Fair
☐ Obtain a list of Campus Clubs
☐ Research and Join Two Campus Clubs
☐ Research Professional Associations
☐ Create an Aspirational Résumé
☐ Review the Job Packet
☐ Obtain Letters of Recommendation
☐ Keep Outstanding Work
☐ Seek Award Opportunities
☐ Create a LinkedIn Account
☐ Attend Two Networking Events
☐ Complete an Informational Interview
☐ Obtain Summer or Part-Time Employment in a Career Field of Choice, or Volunteer in a Career Field of Choice

Chapter Three

Second Year in College

"How puzzling all these changes are! I'm never sure what I'm going to be, from one minute to another."

—Lewis Carroll, *Alice's Adventures in Wonderland*

The goal of the second year in college is to commit to a major and begin making plans for a career. Linking a major to a career requires some thoughtful work. Career opportunities change based upon environmental and technical changes. Researching career trends and mapping the major to your desired career is the goal of your second year.

OVERVIEW

You made it! You successfully completed the first year of college. Transition from high school to college is a challenging process, and you must give yourself a lot of credit for your success.

Now, on to year two! The second year of college is different from the first year. In the first year, there is a little bit of "hand holding" via freshman orientation, student mentors, and freshman events. As a second-year student, there are no events. The college assumes that you understand how college functions; you know the rules and procedures for managing your career; and if you need help or support, you will seek it out. As a second-year student, the choices are many and important.

You are expected to declare a major. What if I don't know what major to choose, then what happens? How do I go about seeking an internship? Should I study abroad; for how long and where? These questions can be

Second Year College Checklist

Work Plan and Skill Assessment	☐ Update the Work Plan ☐ Take a Writing Class
Academic Advising	☐ Obtain Academic Advising
Career Support	☐ Meet with a Career Counselor ☐ Prepare an Elevator Speech ☐ Attend a Career Fair
Academic Clubs and Professional Associations	☐ Run for Club Office ☐ Join Professional Associations
Portfolio	☐ Review Job Packet Information ☐ Obtain Letters of Recommendation, Keep Outstanding Work, Apply for Award Opportunities
Networking	☐ Continue Using LinkedIn ☐ Attend at Least Two Networking Events ☐ Complete Two Informational Interviews
Experience and Employment	☐ Interview Faculty in Career Field of Choice ☐ Shadow Career Professionals ☐ Research Employment Trends ☐ Obtain an Internship, Summer Employment, Part-Time Employment, or Volunteer in Career Field of Interest

overwhelming for some students. The second-year student is held accountable for decisions. You might be afraid to make decisions for fear you might be making a mistake and wasting time.

The goal for the second-year student is to choose a major by the end of the year. In choosing a major, the student "feels" committed to a career direction. For example, if I choose accounting, then I'm going to become an accountant. If I choose finance, then I'm going to be a financial analyst. If I choose education, well of course, I'm going to teach. First, that is not always how it works out. Second, if you do find out in your third year of college that you don't like accounting and do not want to pursue a career in accounting, don't give up! In fact, the good news is that you found out some valuable information: *I'm going to look for a field of interest, or I don't like studying accounting.*

Also, the student support system has changed. Parents assume that the student is making strides in college and enjoying the journey. There are fewer trips home. Friends from high school are pursuing their own journey and are not at home. While the college student is making new relationships at college, it doesn't feel the same. Most students are disappointed by the change.

One important concept in the career planning process that is often missed by self-help books is to understand the changing job market. What jobs are going to be in demand in ten, twenty, or thirty years? Technology is constantly changing the job market. While you may think you know about the job you would like to do, there are many other possibilities within fields of interest.

Give up the notion that all decisions you make must be perfect and that you will choose a major and obtain a career in that field of choice. Rather, continue the exploration of taking courses of interest, schedule coffee dates with people you want to meet, attend events and start conversations with people you don't know, and enjoy the journey.

Let's look at the checklist in detail.

WORK PLAN AND SKILL ASSESSMENT

☐ **Update the Work Plan**

Create a new tab in the work plan for year two. List all of the new tasks in the Excel spreadsheet listed in the checklist for year two. Then, assess those tasks that were not completed in year one and decide if you want to complete or will not complete them. Add those tasks that you want to complete to the new spreadsheet. For those that you don't want to complete, just understand why and move on. Don't let any task become an obstacle to navigating your way through college with the goal of graduating and making strides in pursuing a career or attending graduate school.

☐ **Take a Writing Class**

Communication skills include reading, listening, nonverbal, speaking, and writing skills. Effective writing skills are used throughout college, a necessity for the job search, and essential for career advancement.

The digital age has impacted the writing skills of students. Texts, instant messages, Facebook posts, and blog entries can obscure or distort the message to the receiver.

Because the messages are so cryptic, it sometimes takes several back-and-forth messages to complete the intent. This is not a "bad" issue. The problem arises for students in knowing the difference between writing for social media and using proper English and grammar skills for all other types of writing— the difference between a casual writing style and a more formal writing style.

Companies and businesses expect their employees to write well. Most workers write their own messages and communicate with others through written messages. Today, e-mail is the most common form of communication for workers. Because the employee represents the company, it is important that a professional image is projected all of the time.

Writing well is a skill that must be learned. By enrolling in a writing class, you are taking the first step to improving this communication skill. Learn grammar fundamentals and write. Have teachers critique your writing and understand the areas in which you are weak in order to improve. The better you write, the more you will want to write. Many students state, "I can't write" or "I don't write well." This excuse doesn't work well in the real world. Take the time NOW to learn how to write, and use your college courses to gain experience in writing well. Ask for feedback to improve your writing.

Excellent communication skills will set you apart from other job candidates. In a fast-paced, competitive, and highly connected digital workplace, knowing how to communicate well is more important than ever before.

ACADEMIC ADVISING

☐ Obtain Academic Advising

The second-year goal is to select a major and join a department. With the support of the academic advisor, you will connect with faculty within your selected major. The academic advisor is in a position to assist you in choosing a faculty advisor; but it is important to have an indication of a major, interests, and goals to be directed toward a specific faculty advisor. Faculty advisors are requested based upon mutual interests of the student and professor.

Many campuses offer a "Majors Fair," where all resources are brought together in one place to provide an overview of all majors or programs available to students on campus. Attend the fair and review all programs of interest. By the end of the year, you'll come to a decision regarding a major area of study.

An academic advisor can assist you in incorporating global and civic engagement opportunities into your academic plan. As an option, you can explore opportunities to study abroad or on another campus for a semester or year.

(Note: Study-abroad programs should be explored in the second year to be completed in the third year. Although these programs can be completed in any year, most students want to complete their senior year on campus.)

The sophomore year is another opportunity to select classes based on interests and passions. Take some risks now; if you have an interest in a class, now is the time to consider all options, so you make a wise choice on a major.

CAREER SUPPORT

☐ Meet with a Career Counselor

You will continue the relationship with the career counselor you chose to work with in your first year of college. The career counselor is another person on campus to assist you in making career choices and set realistic plans. The career counselor is knowledgeable of workshops and career-related activities offered specifically for sophomores. Visits to the career counselor at least twice during the second year of college are entries in your work plan.

☐ Prepare an Elevator Speech

An important skill when interviewing, networking, or attending business events is the "elevator speech." An elevator speech is a 30- to 60-second introduction of yourself: name and current status, achievements, and special skills and qualities you bring to the job opportunity.

a) Name and Current Status

Step one in the elevator speech is to introduce yourself and give your current status. Extend your hand and use the techniques discussed in the section *Realize the Importance of a Good Handshake.*

An example: "I am Jane Smith, a junior psychology major at Kent State University, and President of the Entrepreneurial Club."

b) Achievements

Step two is to stimulate the interest of the listener by stating some of your achievements.

An example: "I just organized a regional meeting inviting over thirty entrepreneurs and sixty students. I am in a class right now where we did a consultation for a social agency. I headed up sub-team assessing customer needs. I ended up writing the report."

c) Special Skills and Qualities

Step three is to highlight, to the listener, the special skills and qualities that you offer a potential employer.

An example: "The skills I bring to an organization are initiative, communication, teamwork, and sensitivity to group and individual needs."

d) What Would You Like

The final step in the elevator speech process is to explain clearly what you are seeking. For example, if you are speaking to a hiring manager and interested in an internship, state this fact and ask about the internship program the company offers. If you are interested in an informational interview, state that you will call the individual in a couple of days to inquire about an informational interview. Always request a business card and give the person your business card (the importance of business cards is discussed later in the chapter).

Note: While the elevator speech must be rehearsed, the content must be internalized, not memorized. The elevator speech is not delivered the same way all of the time, as you need to be able to vary the delivery given the circumstance.

The elevator speech provides the opportunity to promote yourself to others. It is a *practiced* speech describing who you are and is often the response to the first question in a job interview. So, practice, practice, and practice. Here's why:

1. There is an old adage that states, "You never get a second chance to make a first impression." Good posture when delivering the elevator speech conveys confidence. Smiling when delivering the elevator speech is essential as it represents approachability and friendliness.
2. When the elevator speech is rehearsed, good verbal skills are exhibited. The use of proper English is imperative, especially during a job interview. Normally, the first question during a job interview is "Tell me about yourself." The answer is repeating the elevator speech.
3. You must practice the elevator speech paying specific attention to speaking in a good tone and speed—not too loud or soft, and not too quickly or slowly.
4. A very easy way to prepare an elevator speech is to record yourself. Most smartphones have the capability to record and playback a video. Keep practicing using this plan until you sound "rehearsed" and you appear confident, articulate, and professional.

☐ Attend a Career Fair

This is your second year attending a career fair. Since career fairs occur each year on campus, and sometimes twice a year, companies usually send the same person: a human resource representative. You want to make an impression at the career fair with specific companies before you need to.

Consider several guidelines for the career fair. First, dress appropriately. Make sure your dress is business casual. You do not have to dress in a suit; however, you don't want to make a negative impression by the way you dress. Second, obtain information about the company and keep this information for when you need it. Companies usually bring flyers for distribution. The information on the flyers is what is meaningful to the company; therefore, this information becomes meaningful to you. Bring the information home and store it in individual folders with the company name on the folder. When applying to companies for a position or interviewing for a job, this information is valuable and accessible.

Next, introduce yourself to the representative from the company. State that you are a second-year student and you are becoming familiar with the career fair process. You are eager to learn about the company and whether the company hires graduates. The idea is to make small talk with the representative, and obtain information about the company.

Finally, network effectively. When you are standing in line or traveling from one booth to the next, engage in conversation with your fellow students. This is an opportunity to obtain contact information and add it to your LinkedIn account.

ACADEMIC CLUBS AND PROFESSIONAL ORGANIZATIONS

☐ Run for Club Office

In the first year of college, you were to join at least two academic clubs on campus. Ideally, you found that participating in these extracurricular activities is fun and you want to continue for the second year. The beginning of the second year is the time to assess whether you enjoyed the club and the club activities interested you or not. Do you "want" or "should" you participate in the club's activities? Be honest. Evaluate your participation in the clubs chosen from the first year and change if the activities are not enjoyable and you are willing to try something different.

You should join at least one club related to your career interest. As you are narrowing in on your career field of interest, join a club that reinforces this area. These are career-building and networking opportunities. These are the type of people who are interested in the same field as you. You are evaluating whether or not you enjoy the people, the topics, and the activities.

Academic clubs offer opportunities to gain experience in a wide range of skills including leadership and management. For example, you can volunteer to find a guest speaker to attend a club meeting. This simple act demonstrates leadership and management skills. If you are interested in the accounting field, then volunteer to be the club's treasurer. To show initiative and separate yourself from other students on campus, run for club office. As a club officer you are in a position to propose and accomplish a range of activities of personal interest and the club's interest.

Researching the clubs on campus, joining a club, becoming an officer, and proposing and hosting events are proactive activities. You are assuming responsibility for your career and activities in support of that choice. What you participate in and contribute to in the clubs of choice are accomplishments. All of these newly developed skills can be included on your résumé as you would if you had a paying job. The good news is employers see it that way, too. Employers are looking to see that you have taken advantage of opportunities on campus in pursuit of a career.

☐   Join Professional Associations

Once you decide on a major, it is important to find professional associations that are affiliated with that major. Many professions have associations, and many have national, state, and local chapters. Refer to Appendix B for a list of many associations affiliated with an area of interest. Do your own research on which organization is the best to join as a student. One way to determine the best organization is to ask a professor in your area of study. For example, if you are interested in marketing, ask your marketing professor.

Check the Internet for information regarding the professional association and the cost for a student. The student rate to join a professional association is a lot less than when you are a professional. Also, check to see if there are local chapters where the group hosts meetings. You want to join an organization where you can attend meetings and begin to network with professionals in the area of interest.

Professional associations host numerous events throughout the year such as conferences, certification workshops, and local chapter meetings. When you attend these events, usually at a lower cost for students, the benefits are many. There are no expectations for students attending events. You are there to participate when you are ready. Just attending events and getting used to the environment is enough for the second-year college student. Recognize the key people in the field. Who writes the articles in your field of study? Who are the presenters at the national or state conferences? You are absorbing all the information about the organization and people at this stage in your career.

When attending professional association events, it is important to create professional relationships by networking. Give yourself a goal to meet three to five new people at every event you attend. Introduce yourself to others and make small talk. This activity becomes easier the more you practice. You want to perfect this skill while still in college.

Another reason to attend professional association events is to learn about news in your career field. Most meetings include an educational aspect to the event. You will enhance your knowledge in the field by listening to the presentations of the key achievers in your field of choice.

Note: When you join a professional organization of interest the vocabulary and information discussed at the meetings could exceed your knowledge level. With taking classes coupled with attending the meetings, you will catch up to the level of the group faster than if you hadn't attended the events. Just stick with attending the meetings. This coupled with attending college courses in the field will provide opportunities to learn the vocabulary in the field at a faster pace.

Professional associations provide resource information that you can use in your course work, too. Most associations provide access to case studies, articles, white papers, and books written by key people in your field of interest. Being able to access this information is a bonus for you, as you learn more about your career interest.

Most associations provide scholarship opportunities for students as well. This is an area worth investigating. You want to learn more about the opportunities and requirements for the scholarships. To reduce the amount of work to apply for a scholarship, you may consider completing a class assignment related to the requirements for the scholarship. You can ask your professor for feedback prior to submitting this body of work in support of the requirement.

So in the second year of college, the goals are to join a professional organization, attend local events, begin to network with people in your field, become familiar with the key achievers in your field, and educate yourself on the opportunities available for the college student.

PORTFOLIO

Refer to Table 2.2.

☐ Review Job Packet Information

The job packet consists of a résumé and cover letter written specifically for a job advertisement. A list of stellar references, usually three, plus business cards complete the job packet. During your second year, you will review the information required to complete a job packet, specifically the résumé and stellar references.

In preparation for writing an excellent résumé, become familiar with the résumé sections:

- Objective: A statement to indicate to the employer the specific job advertisement you are applying to.
- Summary of qualifications: A summary or highlights of the qualifications or skills you bring to a job.
- Education: A chronological listing of colleges attended. You do not have to list high school information on a résumé.
- Work experience: Work experience significant and relevant to the position you are seeking. You are targeting the job advertisement by stating the skills and qualifications you possess for the job.
- Memberships: Professional associations you are affiliated with are listed in this section.
- Optional: Include awards, scholarships, fellowships, dean's list, honors, recognition, commendations, and certificates in this section.

As you navigate through college, your job is to look for ways to enhance your résumé. You seek opportunities to complete the sections of your résumé. You want to gain experience and skills in your targeted area to satisfy the important "keywords" that employers within your field are seeking; keywords you hear at networking events and meetings of professional associations.

To provide evidence of your potential by including successful talents achieved throughout college is the goal for the college student. By including activities in many different organizations, you demonstrate that you are a well-rounded person with leadership and interpersonal skills.

☐ Obtain Letters of Recommendation, Keep Outstanding Work, and Apply for Award Opportunities

In your first year of college, a goal was to obtain letters of recommendation from individuals, such as instructors, your current employer or previous employers, colleagues or subordinates, and other professional contacts. The "stellar" references are selected from these letters of recommendation obtained. These are individuals willing to discuss your qualifications and to give you a glowing or "stellar" endorsement. Personal friends, family, or neighbors are not included in the stellar reference list. Companies are interested in the opinions of those individuals who know how you perform professionally and academically.

In your second year, you want to review the work you saved in your first year of college and add to it. Employers want to know specifically what you can do for their companies. Therefore, do you have examples of your special skills? If you are proficient in computers, do you have an example that you can present during an interview? You want to collect examples that highlight your initiative, dependability, responsibility, resourcefulness, leadership, and management skills. Continue to keep outstanding work and seek opportunities relevant to your targeted job. Include examples of your writing, speaking, and presentation skills. If you worked on a team project, that too should be saved. This demonstrates to employers that you can work successfully on a team.

Finally, you want to look for opportunities to separate yourself from others and to showcase your unique skills, such as awards you have won, workshops attended, certificates earned, honors awarded, and any other accomplishment in college. There are many opportunities to win awards. So, run for office of a club, apply for scholarships, and participate in college competitions for the chance to include the award on your résumé. Employers like to see these types of awards on graduates' résumés. To apply for an award takes a one-page narrative on why you should win. Keep enhancing this document and apply to as many awards as you have the time. If you don't win, don't fret; keep applying. This is a win–win opportunity.

NETWORKING

☐ **Continue Using LinkedIn**

You need to complete the following sections for your LinkedIn profile with as much details known to you, and keep updating, as more information becomes known. Also, as you begin to expand your network and obtain contact information through attending networking events, add contacts to LinkedIn.

- Photo: Your photo should be a headshot in front of a plain background. Don't forget to smile, as it shows friendliness.
- Headline: The headline should state what your major is or what you are interested in pursuing. For example: Economics Major and Aspiring Financial Analyst.
- Summary: The summary is very similar to your elevator speech. Describe yourself, what your skills are, and what you will be doing next.
- Experience: You will list the jobs you held, full-time, part-time, or volunteer work. State your accomplishments in each job. You can attach photos and videos from your work, too.

- Organizations: You should join at least two clubs on campus, and include them under the Organizations tab. Have you joined a club outside of school? Include that, too. Describe what you did with each organization.
- Education: Starting with college, list all your educational experiences, including summer programs.
- Volunteer experiences: Be sure to list all volunteer jobs with a brief description of your work.
- Skills and expertise: List at least five key skills, and then your connections will start endorsing you. Some of the skills could include leadership, communications, management, and the like.
- Honors and awards: If you have earned an honor or award, this is the area to list it.
- Courses: List the classes that are related to your career field or major; do not list all of the courses you have taken.
- Projects: Talk about significant projects meaningful to you. Did you lead a team? Did you present at a school function?
- Recommendations: Over time, you will request managers, professors, or classmates who have worked with you to write a recommendation.

☐ Attend at Least Two Networking Events

Do you consider yourself a shy person? If so, being out of work trumps being shy. If you want a career and a job, you must overcome being shy.

If you are a shy person, if talking to people you don't know is frightening, or if you feel too scared to network effectively, it is time to GET OVER IT! The first step in successful networking is to practice the elevator speech. You must be ready to confidently talk about yourself, your background, and what type of job you are seeking. Being confident will make talking to others easier. Remember, you are not asking for a job when networking. You are telling people you are seeking a job. In year two in college, you are using your elevator speech to meet people and get contact information. Once you have obtained contact information, you add that individual to your LinkedIn account.

There is good news. The more you deliver your elevator speech, the easier it becomes. It just takes practice and perseverance. As you attend events, make it a point to meet at least four people every four months and obtain their contact information to add to LinkedIn. Some potential networking events to pursue in this year include:

- Place you live: people within your geographical area.
- School you attend: fellow classmates, professors, and the like.

- Workplace or volunteer: fellow employees; meet people in the area you would like to pursue.
- Activities and hobbies: places where you normally spend your free time: the gym, sport activities, book clubs, and the like.
- Religious or community groups: places where you worship offer opportunities to gather with others.
- Your day-to-day activities: waiting for public transportation, getting your hair styled, standing on line for coffee, going to the movies, and so on.

Why, these aren't real networking events, you may say. Well, yes they are. You want to make connections and keep in contact with people whom you see on a regular basis. Networking means meeting and connecting to people on an informal basis, before you need them. Also worth noting, people you connect with will need you, too. Networking is a give-and-take relationship between people. There will come a time in your professional career when you will give back and help the people in your network.

☐ Complete Two Informational Interviews

As you start to narrow down the possibilities of choosing a major, an informational interview is a good way to make a contact in your major. At this stage in your career journey, informational interviews should be interesting. As you narrow in on a major, more questions should arise and asking those questions is the purpose of the informational interview. And, people want to help! So, pick up the phone or e-mail a contact to schedule an informational interview.

Ask about the interviewer's career path and experiences. You want to know what the responsibilities are for the specific job held by the individual. Discuss the work environment; is it a relaxed culture or more structured? What are the advantages and disadvantages of working for this particular industry or company?

While the meeting may be casual and you begin to develop a friendly relationship, don't be misled. The interviewer is very serious about their position and career. Most people take their jobs seriously and will not speak negatively about people or the company; therefore, respect that person's position, time, and create the best possible impression that you can. Dress appropriately, offer to pay for coffee or lunch, and maintain professionalism throughout the interview. Many informational interviews turn into internships or part-time positions. Treat the experience in a professional manner.

EXPERIENCE/EMPLOYMENT

☐   Interview Faculty in Career Field of Choice

An employment resource that many students overlook stares you in the face every day: the college professor. In fact, many students are intimidated and don't converse with college professors. Students feel that college professors are too busy or don't care about the students. This is not true—all a myth.

A college professor is more than welcoming to students. All you have to do is schedule an appointment and prepare for your conversation. Write out your questions prior to the appointment. What is it that you want to learn or discuss? You are attending college to choose a major and secure a job after college. What job opportunities are available after graduation before you select this major? This is what you want to determine, and the resources to answer the questions are on campus.

☐   Shadow Career Professionals

One of the best ways to learn about a job is through job shadowing a career professional. Find out what it is like to go to work every day in this particular job, before you actually get there someday. Wouldn't you like to know the answer to this question before you spend time and effort pursuing a career?

Following a person around for a day to learn what the person's job is really like requires some preparation. First, you have to find a person in your field of interest. This should not be too difficult if you completed the informational interviews from years one and two. Another option is to contact the Alumni Center at your college. The center could help you find a person in a major of choice to job shadow. Or, contact a professor in your field of study. Professors have contacts with fellow professionals within various organizations and could facilitate the job-shadowing process.

Once you have an individual to shadow, schedule a day that highlights a daily routine. The first time you shadow someone, you will not have any expectations or know what to request or observe. But, once you complete one job-shadow opportunity, you will soon discover what you want to learn. You should devise a list of questions and information you want to know regarding your next experience. Your goal is to determine if this is the type of job you would be interested in pursuing, once you have graduated.

Over time, by repeating the job-shadow process, you will become savvier in the questions you are asking. What are the opportunities for entry-level employees within this company, or in general? What can you expect when seeking employment in this field, once you have graduated? Most people will open up about the company and position, if asked probing questions. There is a fine balance between talking too much and asking questions, because the objective is to listen to the answers to obtain information. Be careful not to show negative feelings or say anything that can be construed as criticism during the job-shadowing process. The person you requested to job shadow is doing YOU a favor. Respect his or her job, position, and company.

A job shadow is much like going on an interview. You need to know something about the organization, so you are knowledgeable and can display your interest. You need to dress as a professional, arrive on time, and come prepared with a notebook. In the notebook is the list of questions you would like answered. Plus, as you work throughout the day, jot down notes, more questions, the atmosphere or culture of the company, and general impressions. During breaks or lunch, enter into small-talk mode. Get to know the individual more personally, without being too intrusive. Offer to pay for lunch, given the opportunity.

Once the job-shadow event is completed, remember to give that person your contact information and ask to add his or her contact information to your LinkedIn account. Follow up with a thank-you letter or e-mail for the opportunity and provide a sentence or two on what you found to be important completing the job-shadow process. People like to know that they were helpful and made an impact on someone's career.

☐ Research Employment Trends

What types of jobs will be in demand ten years from now? What types of jobs will be obsolete five years from now? These are important questions to answer when deciding on a major and future career choice. Much has changed in the last two decades due to the advancements in technology. There were jobs in demand ten years ago that virtually disappeared. The same is true for jobs in demand today.

How do you determine the most promising jobs for the next decade? You must do research to figure out what types of jobs are going to be in demand. Yes, you should follow your passion and major in a field that interests you. However, there is a fine balance between following your passion and determining if there will be a job once you graduate from college. For example, there are no longer jobs for switch-board operators. Many of you probably don't even know what this is! File clerks or data-entry clerk positions have virtually disappeared. What about post-office positions? Or, bank tellers? Have you been into a bank recently?

Although there may not be positions as bank tellers, more jobs are being created for those who are web-savvy. Due to the advancement in the Internet and technology, global competition increased and placed a huge burden on the survival of small businesses. Baby boomers are retiring; one of the largest groups of people is leaving the workforce at one time. Consider what jobs are required because of this demographic leaving the workforce.

Take the time to do the research now on career trends ten years from now. Deciding on a career that connects your passion with jobs in demand in the future is a win–win opportunity for you!

SMART IDEA:
DON'T WASTE TIME
Whenever possible, include researching employment trends as a topic for a college course paper. Not only will you gain valuable information for your career choice, but you could incorporate the task for a class assignment.

☐ **Obtain an Internship, Summer Employment, Part-Time Employment, or Volunteer Work in Career Field of Interest**

At this point in your college career you need to engage in employment activities that will build skills and experience for your major. If you are interested in internships, summer employment, part-time employment, or volunteer work, the job you want should offer competencies in your career field, not just to get short-term cash. The idea is to obtain jobs to contribute to your skill set. The mind-set from this point forward is to obtain jobs that will enhance your résumé and obtain competences for your major.

As you work in the field of interest in an entry-level or minor position, various other positions within the same field of interest will become known. You may not be interested in the position that you hold now in the company, but may see a job that does interest you currently held by another employee. You are placing yourself in a position to obtain knowledge about the career choice of interest.

Another added benefit of securing a job in your field of interest is networking opportunities. As you intern, volunteer, or work in a field of interest, the people you meet have similar passions; so connect with them by adding them to your LinkedIn profile. When you are ready to look for your first job out of college, these are the people you will contact.

Check It Off!

Review the second year in college checklist. How many activities are you able to Check Off?

- ☐ Update the Work Plan
- ☐ Take a Writing Class
- ☐ Obtain Academic Advising
- ☐ Meet with a Career Counselor
- ☐ Prepare an Elevator Speech
- ☐ Attend a Career Fair
- ☐ Run for Club Office
- ☐ Join Professional Associations
- ☐ Review Job Packet Information
- ☐ Obtain Letters of Recommendation
- ☐ Keep Outstanding Work
- ☐ Apply for Award Opportunities
- ☐ Update Your LinkedIn Account
- ☐ Attend Two Networking Events
- ☐ Complete an Informational Interview
- ☐ Interview Faculty in Career Field of Choice
- ☐ Shadow Career Professional
- ☐ Research Employment Trends
- ☐ Obtain an Internship, Summer Employment, Part-time Employment, or Volunteer in Career Field of Interest

Chapter Four

Third Year in College

Door: "Why it's simply impassible!
Alice: Why, don't you mean impossible?
Door: No, I do mean impassible. (*chuckles*) Nothing's impossible!"

—Lewis Carroll, *Alice's Adventures in Wonderland*

The third year in college is about getting ready for the job search. You will create the tools in preparation for the job search, establish goals, and prepare for the job application process. If more self-discovery is needed to establish a direction, this is the time to make the effort. If you are focused on a career path, you want to refine your career plans.

OVERVIEW

There is a lot to complete during the third year in college. You are no longer overwhelmed with the college process; you are a seasoned college student. Composing the documents that you need and learning about the job search process provide a sense of confidence before you begin interviewing for the job you seek. If you completed many of the suggestions in the previous chapters, you are ready to create your *job packet*: your résumé, cover letter, and stellar references.

You design a "personal brand" and business card. You are getting prepared to market yourself to employers. You are going after the job you want; nothing is impossible! You are evaluating your career direction and making adjustments. You are taking the information assembled in years one and two, adding to that information, and branching out (networking!) because you are getting comfortable with the process. You know what to do and you need time to do it!

Third Year College Checklist

Work Plan and Skill Assessment	☐ Update the Work Plan ☐ Assess Job Skills in Related Field of Interest
Academic Advising	☐ Obtain Academic Advising ☐ Explore Graduate School
Career Support	☐ Meet with a Career Counselor ☐ Create a Personal Brand ☐ Realize the Importance of a Good Handshake ☐ Attend Career Fairs
Academic Clubs and Professional Associations	☐ Attain Leadership Role With Campus Clubs ☐ Attend Professional Association Meetings ☐ Join Toastmasters
Portfolio	☐ Prepare a Job Packet ☐ Continue to Obtain Letters of Recommendation, Keep Outstanding Work, Seek Award Opportunities
Networking	☐ Maintain Your LinkedIn Account ☐ Attend at Least Four Networking Events ☐ Complete Two Informational Interviews
Experience and Employment	☐ Research Companies of Interest ☐ Obtain an Internship, Summer Employment, Part-Time Employment, or Volunteer in Career Field of Interest

WORK PLAN AND SKILL ASSESSMENT

☐ Update the Work Plan

Add the tasks not completed in college years one and two to the third tab checklist, year three. Ask yourself, "Why are these tasks not completed?" Was there a lack of time, or effort? What was it that prevented you from completing the tasks? It is necessary to reflect on what you did and what you didn't complete and the why for each.

In your work plan, use this knowledge to set realistic expectations for completion. For example, are you shying away from completing the networking tasks? If so, this highlights an area that needs improvement. We usually complete the tasks that we enjoy doing, and postpone or leave incomplete those tasks that we don't like to do or feel we don't excel. Some of the skills in years one and two are critical to learn, such as networking. So, if you shy away from completing tasks, now is the time to overcome the obstacles.

Enter the tasks for year three: task number, approximate start and end dates, and notes for each task. You may want to check the Career Center calendar for workshops and career fair dates to add to the work plan. Time management and organizational skills are significant in this year. Evaluate how you managed your time in the last two years and reevaluate these efforts.

The third and fourth college years are more challenging and demanding of your time. Be mindful of the tasks and schedule them accordingly. The job search will progress more smoothly if you're organized and keep to a schedule.

☐ Assess Job Skills in Related Field of Interest

The job advertisement is the first step in a recruitment process designed to attract qualified candidates for a job, and is usually created by human resource professionals to recruit new staff. A job title is a term that describes the position held by an employee in a few words or less. Depending on the job, the title can describe the job responsibilities, the level of the job, or both. For example, if you are seeking an entry-level accountant position when you exit college, you should do an Internet search for this particular job title. You can search www.occupationalinfo.org/onet/ or www.bls.gov for job titles.

Job titles are not "standard." That means job titles change based upon the company's job advertisement; so it's necessary to read the duties and descriptions to get an idea of the types of jobs and what they are called. The information you acquire from the advertisements is important because the skills or job qualifications employers are seeking for that particular job title will be specified. After reading multiple advertisements, the skills or qualifications you must pursue, while in college, are written in the job advertisements.

For example, the job advertisement for an entry-level accountant position states that the job candidate must know "10-key." When you read multiple job advertisements for the same type of position, the same skill is requested or required. Now is the time to learn this particular skill.

Another example: The job advertisement for an entry-level programmer position specifies that the job candidate must know "Java." However, another job advertisement might state that the job candidate must know "C++."

What is important to note is that the candidate must know a programming language. It is not required that the job candidate know "all" programming languages. But, if you can list on your résumé that you know one programming language, then you can learn more languages. Eventually, you will learn the language specified by the hiring company.

SMART IDEA:

DON'T WASTE TIME

Are you applying for a job with the correct skill set? If not,
what would it take to obtain that skill? Identify classes needed
for the job position that you seek. If specialized certification is
required for the job position that you seek, now might be the
good time to pursue this certification.

There are companies that pay for certifications or graduate
school as part of their benefits package. If this is an interest,
you might want to do some research.

The skills or qualifications that appear regularly on job advertisements
for the job title you seek require your attention now. Search for classes or
workshops that offer this particular skill and schedule to take the class or
workshop. Or, if you have a part-time job, ask your manager if you can gain
experience in this area. Schedule these tasks now, before you start applying
for employment positions. These are new entries to your work plan based
upon the job titles and job advertisements you view. Table 4.1 lists areas, with
descriptions and examples, on the Internet to find job advertisements.

Table 4.1.   Job Advertisement Databases

Areas	Description	Examples
Job boards or big boards	A job board is a website that posts jobs supplied by employers.	CareerBuilder.com Monster.com CollegeGrad.com Indeed.com
Company sites	Online job board specific to a particular company.	
Niche sites	A niche site aggregates job listings in a specific industry, career field, or type of position.	Technology: Dice.com Accounting: Accountemps.com Teaching: Quintcareers.com
Industry-specific sites	These sites are available to search job advertisements by a particular industry or field of interest.	Human Resources: shrm.org Project Management: Careerhq. pmi.org/jobs
Nonprofit sites	These organizations are developed to help others and are not structured to make a profit or redistribute the profit back into the business.	Encore.org Idealist.org Nonprofittalentmatch.com

(Continued)

Table 4.1. *Continued*

Areas	Description	Examples
Government sites	These databases are for government jobs: federal, state, city, or county.	Usajobs.gov, Federalgovernmentjobs.us Govtjobs.com
Career Center job site or Alumni Services job site	Most college Career Centers have job and internship databases available for students. The database offers access to full-time career positions, part-time jobs, internships, and on-campus work study and student assistant positions.	Specific to the college or university
Social networking sites	Social networking sites are web-based services that allow individuals to create a public profile and a list of users with whom to share connections. Some social networking sites include a job data bank with job advertisements.	LinkedIn.com
Collective sites	These sites draw job postings from numerous online sources and could repeat the listings above.	Indeed.com Simplyhired.com Linkup.com

ACADEMIC ADVISING

☐ Obtain Academic Advising; Explore Graduate School

For the first two years in college, the academic advisor is there to assist with general courses required for graduation and to choose a major. Once a major is chosen, the academic advisor provides guidance on your chosen career path. Advisors can provide advice on selecting concentrations or minors, or advice on graduate school.

The academic advisor, together with a faculty advisor in your major department or program, will help you plan a course program to satisfy major requirements, facilitate independent study, and provide direction based upon students' interests.

While all of these programs are available to those who commit to a major, don't be afraid to change your major at this time, too. It is best to meet with an academic advisor to determine the requirements to change a major rather than completing a program in which you no longer have an interest.

You should complete college even though you are not positively 100% sure the major you selected is worth pursuing. There are many people employed in fields unrelated to their major in college. Somehow, someway, it all seems to work out. Talk to your academic advisor, who can help you explore all possibilities before making decisions.

CAREER SUPPORT

☐ Meet with a Career Counselor

Draw upon your career counselor's expertise especially if you have built a good relationship with him or her. There are two important tasks to complete during your junior year with your career counselor: creating your job packet and obtaining internships.

The good news is that you don't have to do these two tasks alone. The career counselor can help you create a great résumé. A résumé is an "iterative" task. That means you create your résumé and tweak it all the time. Once you start creating a résumé, the process does not stop until you retire. It is a personal document that changes continually, as you change. Also, you may have different versions for different purposes. Creating a résumé for the first time is a formidable experience and a huge time commitment. Taking the help of a career counselor makes the process easier (or eases the pain). The Career Center offers résumé-writing workshops and résumé critiques. Take advantage of these services.

Internships are a great way to obtain real-world experience and provide exposure to a career. Internships are short-term work programs, paid or unpaid, to focus on job skills and take what is learned in the classroom and apply it to the real world. Also, this is a good opportunity to realize that this may NOT be the career you are interested in. It is best to learn this now. Employers want candidates with job-related experience.

Also, discuss career trends with the career counselor. Where will the jobs be ten years from now? When trends are identified, you can plan further education and professional development that allows you to keep up with the trends.

Scheduling appointments with a career counselor, writing your résumé, researching internship opportunities, and researching career trends are tasks you should add to the work plan.

☐ Create a Personal Brand

It is a competitive job market. Even if you are successful in attaining a job right out of college, there is no guarantee that you will have that job in five years. You must consider yourself a "contractor" even if you work for a company. Contractors are individuals who work for themselves, offer companies a specific skill set, and get a high hourly wage. Contractors hustle. They work hard, network often, and are always on the lookout for their next job opportunity.

Successful contractors market themselves very well. This strategy is called "branding." Nike, Apple, Microsoft, and Nestle are companies that market well and have a unique brand and logo. You need to start thinking along the same lines about yourself. What is your brand? What are the special skills and abilities you bring to the job market?

To begin your personal branding, all documents in the "job packet" must look the same. The heading, font style, and font size must be the same on all documents. (See Appendix D for sample résumé, cover letters, and stellar references.) This presents a professional image to the company upon presentation.

There are additional ways to create a personal brand:

a. *Professional image.* Company dress codes range from business casuals to business suits. Dress professionally until you know what is acceptable, and pay attention to the details. This means, people notice teeth, jewelry, and nails. Many organizations are conservative and like the employee to adhere to a "proper" dress code. It is better to be overdressed than underdressed. You never know when you will get an opportunity or that "big chance" and you don't want to get caught off guard.

b. *Meet and greet.* It is important to know the "professional" protocol when meeting and greeting other professionals. This starts with the importance of a good handshake, reciting an elevator speech, and giving and asking for a business card.

c. *Online image.* Companies do check the prospective employee's online image. It is important to Google yourself and review what turns up. Creating a professional online image is essential and will be discussed in the next chapter.

☐ Realize the Importance of a Good Handshake

A handshake is an initial connection with and first impression of another person, making this a key activity to learn. People in the United States and various other cultures greet each other with a handshake. In the business environment, first-time meetings between employees of two or more companies are routine. Attending trade shows, conferences, and seminars is common. You should be prepared for this common gesture when meeting people or attending events. (Note: If you suffer from sweaty palms, keep a tissue or hanky in your pocket and wipe your hand just prior to shaking.)

It is imperative to remember the following when shaking hands:

1. Whether shaking hands with a person of the same sex or opposite sex, a firm grip is required. The strength of the grip is firm—not too hard or too weak. A firm grip represents confidence; a weak grip represents lack of self-confidence.
2. Make eye contact and smile during the handshake.
3. When shaking hands, say, "Hi, my name is Jane Smith, and you are? It is very nice to meet you." Also, when possible, add a "hook" or qualifier so the person has something to remember you by. For example, "I'm the person with the curly hair."

☐ Attend Career Fairs (or Job Fairs)

You should feel comfortable and know what to expect attending career fairs, if you attended them in the first two years of college. You should be familiar with the environment and atmosphere. Career fairs are more valuable in the third year of college. Career fairs are hosted by universities, specifically for the college students to meet with a range of employers. You learn a lot about a company in a short period of time. You may be turned on to a company that you did not know existed.

Prior to the date of the career fair, visit your Career Center to find out which companies will be participating. It is important that you do online research of companies, particularly those you don't know, prior to attending the fair. Select those companies that you are interested in and talk with the representative for that company.

The company representative at the career fair is a human resource professional and not the hiring manager. The human resources professional prescreens the job applicants prior to recommending an interview with the hiring manager. First impressions are important.

Dress like a professional. Have your résumé, cover letter, and business cards with you. You have a good handshake and elevator speech prepared. You are ready.

At the company's table or booth, pick up material they provide. Make contact with the human resources professional, shake hands, and deliver your elevator speech. Now is the time to display your knowledge of the company and begin asking questions related to the position you are seeking.

- Hand the human resources professional your résumé and cover letter.
- State the position you are interested in pursuing.
- Inquire as to the hiring process for new graduates. Whom would you call? What is the procedure?

- Ask about the statistics regarding hiring new graduates.
- Ask for the hiring manager's name in the area you are seeking. You may want to do an informational interview.
- Finally, ask for the human resource professional's business card and contact information. Provide yours.

Remember to network at a job fair. Talk to those students waiting in line. Ask questions and listen to the answers. Obtain business cards or contact information.

After the fair, organize the information collected from the fair into folders for each company: electronic or paper. This information will be needed when you start applying for job positions. Add the contact information to LinkedIn. If you are interested in a company, and received the name of the hiring manager, you might consider completing an informational interview at this time. Add these tasks to your work plan to schedule and complete.

ACADEMIC CLUBS AND PROFESSIONAL ASSOCIATIONS

☐ Attain Leadership Role with Campus Clubs

In your third year of college, you should seek a leadership role in a campus club. Demonstrating leadership skills is highly desired by employers and easy to develop by holding a club office. Sometimes, you may be able to assume the leadership of a club because most students don't understand the value of doing so. The single act of holding a club office is beneficial for your résumé. You add to your résumé that you were a club officer and it demonstrates that you have leadership experience.

As you obtain job interviews, the experience gained as a club officer will be beneficial. While on an interview you will be able to tell stories about your leadership experiences. People remember stories better than just facts. What is effective leadership about in today's environment? What are the characteristics and traits that make a good leader? What makes a successful CEO? Many pressures confront leaders in business, government, and nonprofit organizations. Meeting customers' demands, pleasing stockholders, and providing employment are difficulties leaders must manage. Some leaders have a unique personality displaying confidence to solve any issue.

The personality of a leader is significant in the individual's ability to lead. So, what are the traits and qualities leaders possess to manage issues and pressures of the job? Why do some leaders fail and others succeed? These are important questions to answer. Books on the subject can provide some answers, but experience offers insight. That is why it is vital to start small and obtain a leadership role on campus.

One question likely to be asked of job candidates during a job interview is, "Do you have any leadership skills?" Or, "Describe to me a situation where you used your leadership skills to build consensus among group members or to have a successful project." Or, "Give me an example of a time you failed. What happened?" Your answer will be robust, if you assumed a leadership role in college. Every opportunity to undertake a leadership role should be seized.

You learn valuable skills in working with others, leading teams, and being responsible for other people. Many students do not like working in teams because not all students contribute at the same level. Although this may seem discouraging at the time, it provides a valuable leadership lesson for the future.

Having a leadership role also gives you experience in working with different people: diversity in gender, race, religion, or ethnicity as well as differences and preferences. Being a leader is important to an employer because the ability to effectively work well with all types of people is a sought-after skill. Being responsible for a project or coordinating an effort provides leadership stories to share and discuss on an interview. You can state to an interviewer, "This is what I learned when I coordinated our club's networking event on campus."

Leadership experience, acquired as a college student, provides an opportunity to learn how to think quickly, react under stress, pay attention to details, and develop interpersonal and conflict resolution skills. Leadership skills are important to everyone from an employee undertaking simple day-to-day tasks to a CEO managing a corporation. Start learning the skill now!

☐ Attend Professional Association Meetings

During the first two years of college, you attended professional association meetings to get familiar with the association and decide if you had an interest. This is the year to join an association and attend meetings. If it is possible, volunteer to work on a committee. This will help you in several areas.

a. *Network.* The ability to network within an area of interest is the primary goal for attending and volunteering for professional associations. Attend meetings, volunteer for a committee, and network with the members. The members offer advice and provide opportunities. Ask questions to the members regarding where they work, what they do, and where they see opportunities for you after you graduate. These are the people you need to associate with and who provide opportunities in and after college.

b. *Internship and job opportunity.* Often, professional associations offer internship opportunities. Students affiliated with an association are likely to be offered an internship when associated with the organization, which could lead to a part-time or full-time position.

c. *Knowledge.* Volunteering to work on a committee within your chosen field offers many benefits: experience, exposure, and excitement. Being part of a committee provides opportunities like working on a team, learning who the influential people are within the organization, and achieving goals or deadlines. This is very exciting to share and get to know other members of the organization.

d. *Résumé.* If you can include on your résumé that you are a member of the association and volunteered to work on various projects, it improves your profile. It informs the interviewer that you are committed to this career path.

e. *Interview.* Joining an organization, attending meetings, and working on committees provide opportunities to experience your career choice. This information is included on your résumé and provides stories to share during an interview.

□ **Join Toastmasters**

Toastmasters International is an organization that was founded in 1905 to improve the speaking and leadership skills of businessmen. Fast forward to present day and what has changed is "businessmen" to "business people." Toastmasters International has over 14,000 clubs internationally with 313,000 members. Learning and practicing how to speak, conduct meetings, plan programs, and work on committees is still as relevant today as in 1905.

Public speaking is an intimidating experience for the college student. Many college students fear getting up in front of a group of students and presenting, but giving presentations is a learned skill. Once you force yourself to experience this and overcome the fear of presenting, you become confident. When you are confident as a person, it shows. It shows when you are meeting people you don't know at networking events or at a cocktail party. Socializing with others becomes less stressful and a more enjoyable experience.

Colleges are doing a very good job recognizing the importance of teaching public speaking skills. More classes offer students the opportunity to present either individually or as a member of a team. Joining a campus club is another opportunity to practice public speaking skills. Many clubs sponsor lectures or presentations. The more you take opportunities to present, the more comfortable with the process and less nervous you become.

Learning how to present yourself well is a skill that you must master in order to get the job you seek or advance in your career because résumés do not get you the job, interviews get you the job. When you are in the job market, speaking skills rank high on employers' list of skills desired in job candidates. If you have not mastered public speaking, then seek out a Toastmasters club in your area. The by-product of conquering the fear of public speaking is developing self-confidence. What a trade-off!

PORTFOLIO

Refer to Table 2.2.

☐ **Prepare a Job Packet**

A Job Packet includes the following items: (1) Job Advertisement, (2) Résumé, (3) Cover Letter, (4) Stellar References, and (5) Business Cards. Let's discuss the pertinent information on each one of the documents.

1. Job Advertisement

A résumé and cover letter are prepared uniquely for each job advertisement. Read each job advertisement and underline the "keywords." Keywords are words in the job advertisement that relay the job skills and requirements the job applicant should possess.

Since most résumés and cover letters are submitted online rather via mail, the more keywords from the job advertisement placed on the résumé and cover letter, the better chance you will have to be selected for an interview. When you submit a résumé and cover letter online, the information is input to a computer. The computer program compares the job advertisement to the résumés and cover letters. The more "hits" on keywords, the better your chance of the computer selecting your résumé and cover letter. If few or no keywords match between the job advertisement and your résumé and cover letter, then your résumé will not be selected and you will not be offered the opportunity to interview.

College students need to gain experience in their chosen field prior to submitting applications. You must have the skill set required for the position for which you are applying. Review the section (Chapter Four, third year, work plan and skill assessment topic) Access Job Skills in Related Field of Interest for a detailed explanation.

2. Résumé

A résumé is a significant document for the job search. A résumé does not secure you a job; a résumé gets you an interview. The interview gets you the job. (The interview process is discussed in the next chapter.) Employers, especially those who have posted openings on large websites, receive hundreds of résumés for a single position. If your résumé is selected from the numerous résumés posted, then you have written a great résumé.

The following information is EXTREMELY IMPORTANT when you write a résumé. Here are a few ways to get your résumé to the top of the stack.

a. You must read the job advertisement and underline all keywords that describe the qualifications for the specific job for which you are interested in applying.

b. You must show that you are qualified by including as many keywords that describe your qualifications for the desired job in a concise, clear, and attention-getting manner.

c. You must write a professional résumé with no spelling errors and perfect grammar. Also, do not abbreviate or use acronyms. Think PROFESSIONALISM.

d. The physical appearance of the résumé is an important factor and not to be overlooked. It is imperative to create a favorable impression. The résumé must be well organized, concise, and neat.

e. Résumés should not include personal pronouns such as I, me, or my.

Once your résumé is selected by the computer, then it is sent to either a human resource professional or the hiring manager for review. It is their responsibility to review the résumés, looking for the perfect job candidate.

> SMART IDEA:
>
> DON'T WASTE TIME
>
> Usually, the college Career Center offers help in writing a résumé. Spend time with a career counselor to seek input on writing a spectacular résumé. You don't need to do this alone!

The following are the elements to include to write that GREAT résumé:

Organization. You will write a "chronological résumé." A chronological résumé is most frequently used and lists work experience in reverse chronological order, outlining your job history from the most recent job backwards, with greater emphasis on the most recent job. Most employers will ask questions regarding your work experience year by year. So, gaps in the employment history are highlighted clearly in a chronological résumé and must be explained to an employer when interviewing.

The sections of a résumé include heading, professional objective, summary of qualifications, education, and work experience. Optional sections included are memberships, scholarships, activities, military experience, and the like.

Heading. Your name, address (no longer needed), telephone numbers (mobile phone), and e-mail address are placed in the heading on a résumé. Your name font size should be slightly larger than the other information in the heading. As stated in Chapter Two, use your professional e-mail address and phone numbers. Prior to sending the first résumé to a potential employer, verify your voice-mail message and all communication methods listed on your résumé are professional.

Professional objective. Most often, you are sending a résumé and cover letter in response to a specific job advertisement. If this is the case, your objective statement is very easy. You need to read the job advertisement and underline the specific name of the job title. If there is an associated job number with the job title, underline that as well. Once done, the objective statement reads:

"Seeking the {job title} position for {company name}; job number {include the job number}."

Done! The objective statement is very simple and clear.

If you are not writing a résumé in response to a specific job advertisement, then the objective statement is written differently. One example where a résumé without a specific job title is useful is at a job fair. When handing out résumés at a job fair, you want a more generic objective statement because you will be handing out your résumé to various companies.

The onus is on you to know what type of job you are seeking. If you know the position you are seeking, then state the position, for example:

"Seeking an entry-level accounting position for your organization."

If you do not want to be that specific, you can state the opportunity you are seeking in a more generic way:

"Seeking an entry-level position in your financial department to contribute strong analytical skills, education, and experience to your organization."

The purpose of an objective statement is to state the specific position you are seeking for the person reviewing the résumé. If you are submitting the résumé electronically, it is vital that you use the same terminology that is on the job advertisement as these are keywords.

Summary of qualifications statement. The summary of qualifications section is a three- to eight-item bulleted list that summarizes your experience, areas of expertise, traits, or distinguishing characteristics to separate you from every other candidate applying for the same position. This is another section in the résumé where you need to use the keywords that match the job advertisement.

Use as many of the keywords from the job advertisement on your résumé that apply to you, as employers are seeking those keywords! The more keywords used, the better your résumé reads. If the job advertisement states that the company is looking for someone with excellent communication skills, then your bulleted item will read "Excellent oral and written communication skills."

Education. List your educational background in reverse chronological order including your highest degree and university first, and include the anticipated graduation date (this shows you are goal oriented). State the exact name of the university rather than the nickname or short version of the university name.

The standard protocol on writing a résumé is to list your grade point average (GPA) only if it's a 3.0 or higher. If the GPA in your major is over a 3.0, then list "major GPA" on your résumé. You can list both if over 3.0.

Employment history with accomplishments. Employment history includes company names, years employed, job titles, and responsibility or accomplishment statements. This is the section that is most difficult for students to write. And, this is the section where you could get help from the Career Center. Draft the responsibility or accomplishment statements first and then take your résumé to the Career Center to edit.

- Responsibility statements summarize information from your job description, special assignments, and general duties that a potential employer would find to be of interest.
- Accomplishment statements show achievements and contributions to the organization—three to six for a recent job, and one to three for prior jobs.

The responsibility/accomplishment statement is a three-part statement written in a specific format: *action verb, what did you do, and with what result.* Refer to Table 4.2 there are "action verbs" listed on the Internet that provide ideas when writing the statement. Do not use the same action verb all the time. "What did you do" is easy to write for most people; it is specific and descriptive of the functions of the job. It is "with what result" that most people leave out or do not write particularly well. This is the quantitative

Table 4.2.   Examples of Elements of the Responsibility/Accomplishment Statement

Action verb	What did you do?	With what result or impact?
Wrote	Technical manual for a new software product	Resulted in high commendations from executives
Organized and conducted	A fund-raising gala	Resulted in $10,000 more than last year's gala

section of the statement. For example, a statement that is written, "Sold forty cars" is not impressive; but written as, "Sold forty cars, which is 20% more than peers" is now impressive.

Most students, as well as professionals writing a résumé, omit the third section of the accomplishment statement. When this section is omitted, then the statements are generalized and appear as every other person holding the same job would write. The "with what result" section is important and do not omit when writing a résumé to separate yourself from every other job candidate.

These statements are central to the résumé. This is the main section in the résumé where you must use the KEYWORDS from the job advertisement. You need to show that your education and experience match the skills needed in the job advertisement.

Other sections. The following sections are optional on résumés. However, these are the sections that differentiate you from the other hundreds of job candidates. Paying attention to these sections is as essential as the other mandatory sections. Include memberships and offices held in professional associations, clubs on campus, and community activities. These activities should relate to the position you are seeking.

Do not list activities that are not related to the job you are seeking. Do not list activities from high school or pure enjoyment activities unless you received awards or honors. For example, if you are a beach volleyball player and enjoy this sport tremendously, it isn't relevant if you are applying for a programming position in a high-tech firm. However, if you won national titles in the sport, then that is impressive to the employer. It demonstrates fortitude and dedication. Please review the 15 most common resume mistakes in Box 4.1.

To separate yourself from others, you want to list notable accomplishments or achievements. If you won a scholarship, competition, or award, then include these accomplishments. Include any leadership activity on your résumé.

- Memberships
- Honors
- Activities (community, volunteer)

- Scholarships
- Military

(Please see Appendix D for sample résumé, cover letters, and reference templates.)

Final notes. A résumé is a formal professional document and must be written with a certain protocol, as outlined here. A print-based résumé is brought to the job interview, for person-to-person networking, for career fairs, or a job that does not require an electronic version. There are some other noteworthy requirements:

- *Check spelling and grammar.* (This point is important.)
- Use Times New Roman or Calibri font with a 12-point font size.
- Use black font color on a white background.
- Be creative to modify the format but stay within the professional limitations.
- Limit your resume to two pages. The most important feature to consider when writing a résumé is the "white space" on the page; keep this to a minimum. If there is too much "white space," then your résumé is a candidate for a one-page résumé.
- Pay attention to the page break on a two-page résumé. You should have the page break at a good location, completing one area before moving on to another. Include your name and page number on the second page; no need to repeat the heading.
- E-mail your résumé to yourself to verify the settings. You don't want the settings to move once delivered. Note: You could convert the document to a .pdf file. This is a readable version on most computers.

When submitting a résumé via online or digital submission, specific formatting rules must be followed. You convert the print-based résumé to a plain-text résumé, so that it is available for e-mailing or pasting into online résumé submission forms. After you complete the changes, e-mail the résumé to yourself to view prior to sending it to an organization. Read the job advertisement carefully, as there may be instructions on how to submit an online résumé. The following are changes generally required:

- Use standard 8 1/2" × 11" white paper.
- Use Times New Roman or Calibri (use ordinary fonts).
- Use 12-point font size (10 or 14 is acceptable too).
- Remove images, designs, colors, graphics, tables, charts, and the like.
- Remove page breaks.
- Replace bullets with asterisks or plus signs.
- In MS Word, save the document with Plain Text (*.txt) as the file type.

BOX 4.1   THE 15 MOST COMMON RÉSUMÉ MISTAKES

1. Not realizing that the résumé is a business proposal; believing that it gets you the job.
2. Failing to back it up with other approaches to job search.
3. Thinking that one size fits all—sending out the same old résumé regardless of the job, failing to tailor it to what the employer needs.
4. Failing to research what the employer wants.
5. Exceeding the two-page limit or cheating by reducing the type size and fiddling with the margins. The proper length for a résumé is 500–600 words. If the résumé is too long, the solution is to reduce the word count, not to reduce the type size.
6. Writing about responsibilities not achievements; not realizing that the employer's question is always, *So what? So what did you add? If you just did your job, that's not interesting.*
7. Putting the least interesting material on the first page, for example, qualifications, training courses.
8. Giving a lot of irrelevant data: date of birth or age, driving license status, marital or health status, listing all the training courses the person has attended.
9. Using feeble language, for example, modifiers such as *rather, quite, very,* or bland words like *got* or *did* instead of powerful words like *led* or *improved.*
10. Using management jargon: *blue sky thinking, strategic envelope, going offline, roll-outs, moving the goal posts, stepping up to the plate.*
11. Writing a personal profile which could describe anyone, for example, using words such as *professional, lively, self-motivated.*
12. Describing personal interests that could be anyone's: *hiking, walking, reading, cooking, being with family.*
13. Lying: upgrading qualifications, improving salary, forging references, making previous job duties sound more important than they were or are.
14. Failing to convey a strong personal brand—wanting to be "safe."
15. Not realizing that employers will check out a résumé on the Internet and failing to manage Internet presence carefully.

Source: Used with permission from Jenny Rogers.

---

3. Cover Letter

The cover letter is not your résumé. Many students, when writing a cover letter, reiterate the facts from the résumé because they don't know what else to write. Cover letters provide a great opportunity for you to market yourself. Once again, the cover letter is another opportunity to include the keywords from the job advertisement. These are the two most important questions that must be answered in the cover letter and often omitted by job applicants:

1. Why do you want to work for this particular organization?
2. Why are you suitable for this position?

The cover letter is not a generic letter sent to every organization to which you are applying. The cover letter is a unique letter for each organization and must be personalized. It implies that you know something about the company for which you are applying. Most often, the person you are submitting your résumé to is included on the job advertisement. Underline this name. Find out the specific title for this individual (use the Internet or phone the company) and include the name and title on the letter. Verify the company's full name and address. Don't assume you know the name of the company. For example, it is The Walt Disney Company, not Disney Co.

If the name of the person you are submitting to is not included within the job advertisement, then address the letter to the Director of the Human Resources Department.

When you are writing the cover letter, it is your task to state what skills you offer and how you can contribute to the company's success. State what you can do for the company, not what the company can do for you. Focus on character traits as opposed to tasks or skills. If the advertisement wants someone who is a good communicator, give a demonstration of how you have effectively used your communication skills.

The cover letter is a business letter. There is a specific format for business letters. Please see Appendix D for a sample cover letter and follow the format. Cover letters should have the same font style and font size as the résumé. Also, cover letters should not exceed one page in length. Keep it short, concise, and clear. Once again, it is very important that you edit for spelling and grammatical errors.

One more fact regarding cover letters: If you are applying to a company online via e-mail, do not attach the cover letter. Instead, place the cover letter in the e-mail and attach your résumé; the person receiving the cover letter and résumé will not take the time to open the attachment. (Note: It is a good idea to attach the cover letter as well as imbed it within the e-mail.)

The information that must be included in the cover letter is outlined in the following sections. The cover letter is divided into three sections, which could encompass one or more paragraphs.

First section. In your opening paragraph, state the position for which you are applying. This information is taken right from the job advertisement. Next, state how you learned about the position. If you heard about the position from someone who works for the organization, be sure to mention his or her name, department, and the like. Finally, answer one of the two important questions for a cover letter: Why do you want to work for this particular organization?

In order to obtain this information you could (a) do research on the Internet about the organization, (b) visit the company or company stores (if that is the case) to learn about the company, (c) review the company's website, and/or (d) use your social network contacts. Ask your social network contacts via LinkedIn or Facebook for an acquaintance who has worked or works for this company, and then invite this person out for coffee or lunch for an informational interview. Find out all you need to know about the organization from someone who has knowledge about the organization.

Second section. In the next paragraph or two, give a brief introduction of yourself and your background. Explain your interests that match the job description and the organization. Illustrate how your experiences align with the job description. This could include work, school, volunteer, church, experience, and the like. Use the keywords in the job description. Your task is to make it easy for the employer to see a match between you and the job. You are answering the second important question for the cover letter: Why are you suitable for this position?

Third section. In the last paragraph, state that you will contact the company in two weeks to schedule an interview. Express your appreciation to the person to whom you are directing the letter and your eagerness to discuss the employment opportunity. End the letter with a closing statement, salutation, and your name. If you are mailing the letter, write your name legibly. Note: There are times when the company does not provide the contact information or requests not to be contacted. This request must be respected. Refer to Box 4.2.

4.   Stellar References

Most companies check references after an interview and only if the company is considering you for the position. Therefore, it is not necessary to give out your references prior to the company requesting them. *Do not* list references on your résumé or state "references available upon request."

Your task is to prepare a list of stellar references: names, titles, phone numbers and e-mail addresses, and how you are linked to these individuals. These are three to five individuals who will provide a "glowing" recommendation of your work. How do you know that this individual will provide this glowing recommendation? Well, you have to ask him or her. The question you ask is, "Will you be a stellar reference for me?" Due to the competition of job applicants, it is imperative that you know what your stellar reference will say about you. Once the individual has agreed to be a stellar reference, ask how he or she would like to be contacted by the organization via e-mail or phone. Obtain the information to include on your stellar reference list.

The recommendation must be a glowing endorsement of your skills and abilities. The people you ask will be former or current employers (manager or

---

BOX 4.2 COVER LETTERS DOS AND DON'TS

Do

1. The best cover letters reveal your enthusiasm for a particular job and the employer and tell the employer why you are worthy of consideration.
2. Personalize your cover letter by addressing your letter to a specific individual (better chance of being read).
3. Highlight your most impressive strengths and experience but leave the detailed chronological listing of your prior employment to your résumé.
4. Make sure your letter looks professional.
5. Keep your letter to one page.
6. Put your cover letter in the body of the e-mail, not as an attachment.
7. Techniques:
   - Use headlines.
   - Use lists (with bullet points).
   - Use a quotation.
   - Include a testimonial.
   - Describe a problem and solution.
   - Ask a question.
   - Provide a notable example.
   - Be bold. Add two sentences that best describe you.

Don't

1. Send a résumé without a cover letter.
2. Use lingo, emoticons, and jargon.
3. Mark your e-mail "urgent."
4. Be afraid to send follow-up cover letters:

   "I'm writing again because I know I have the skills and great attitude you seek. I'm sending you this second letter to demonstrate my genuine enthusiasm and to again request an interview."

   "I applied for the position of [insert position] about 10 days ago. I'm following up because I know I have the ability and experience that the position requires."

Source: Used with permission from Jenny Rogers.

---

above in position), coaches, professors, directors of volunteer organizations, or other professional contacts. Friends, family, clergy, or neighbors are not considered professional references and should not be considered.

Equip your reference with as much information as possible, so that the reference is prepared when contacted by the company. Provide your stellar reference with a copy of your résumé and cover letter when you obtain an interview. Your reference needs information on what the "keywords" are for this particular job application, so that he or she can offer the best endorsement of your qualifications for the specific job.

5.　*Business Cards*

A business card (or calling card) is still used in today's networking environment. A business card provides tangible information for the people you meet when you are going to networking events, such as professional association meetings, or standing in line at Starbucks and happen to talk to someone with whom you would like to keep in contact.

When introducing yourself to others, have your business card ready to hand to the person. It makes you look professional. After the encounter, it is a good idea to write a note or two on the reverse side of the card about the individual you met, so that you can remember and follow up at a later time. Recently, a student went to her first networking event and said, "people were handing their business cards out like it was candy!"

Many students say, "Well, I have a smartphone and it is very easy to collect contact information this way instead of obtaining business cards." This is very true and is a viable option in today's technological environment. There are "apps" out there where you can share information easily with someone. Yes, this is an alternative and probably will replace the business card, in the future. There are times when you won't have time to enter the contact information into your phone; so it is easier to hand the person a business card. It is best to be prepared. Note: Fidgeting with your phone doesn't scream "professional;" it says "not prepared."

The point in handing someone a business card is for "networking." Would you rather take the two minutes talking to the person by entering contact information into your phone, or use the time to make a first impression? Business cards are a means to exchange information in a professional manner. It is a one way to show you are a professional in the game of conducting business.

In addition, a business card is one way to distinguish you from others. It is a technique in branding you. Most companies you work for provide business cards. If not, design one yourself and have it printed by a website such as www.vistaprint.com.

- Use a white card, print on the front, and leave the back blank. This way, people can write notes on the back of the card.
- The traditional business card is a standard size of 2" by 3.5". Stick with this protocol.

- Include your name, e-mail, and phone number (optional). Some people include their picture on the business card. This is helpful as a reminder.
- If you are a student, you can list your college or university and major.
- In keeping with the "personal branding theme," have the card resemble your job packet theme. Use the same font style as the job packet and at least a 12-point font size.
- While many companies offer business cards for little cost, be careful that the card does not look cheap when printed on inexpensive paper. This is not a message you want to convey to people you meet.

☐ Continue to Obtain Letters of Recommendation, Keep Outstanding Work, and Seek Awards and Scholarship Opportunities

In previous chapters, the importance of asking for and keeping letters of recommendation, examples of your work throughout college, and award certificates or scholarships was presented. This continues through your third year.

This is the year to seek opportunities in the classroom to add to your body of work. Review what you have kept in your first two years of college. Is the work good enough to present during an interview? Do you have an example of good writing skills? How about a presentation example using PowerPoint? Have you done statistical work in college where you used Excel? Take the time in your courses to work on papers and projects to add to your portfolio.

NETWORKING

☐ Maintain Your LinkedIn Account

There are two schools of thought when participating in social network sites: (a) connect with people you know versus (b) connect with anyone and everyone. As stated in Chapter One, your internal network is more effective personally and professionally than your external network. The strategy to networking is to meet more people (external network) and know them well enough to move to your internal network. More is *not* better; stress quality over quantity.

As you begin attending more networking events and meeting people, you will begin requesting business cards and contact information. These are the people you will add to your LinkedIn account. These are people who have similar interests and concentrations. Keep searching for new individuals you know and add them to your LinkedIn network.

LinkedIn has a "groups" feature. There are groups for alumni, associations, nonprofits, professional interests, corporations, general networking, conference attendees, and personal interests. This is a feature of the website worth exploring, if you have not done so already.

More companies are adding a corporate profile on LinkedIn. Once you attend career fairs, or are interested in a specific company, choose to "follow companies" on LinkedIn. This will give you automatic updates on changes or updates when posted by the company. You are now "tapped in" to automatic updates on changes to the company. This can include an array of information from company mergers, hiring, downsizing, leadership changes, new products, new stores, and the like.

There is a limit to the number of groups you can join per account holder. At one time, the limit was fifty. This can change; so please do your own research. You want to join groups that provide you the most value and help you meet your goals. Once again, as the navigation to view and select groups is updated, you want to view the site and figure it out. The process is to search the directory for potential groups to join; you could enter the name of a company, school, professional association, skill, or hobby. Once you narrow the search, read the group's description. Some groups require you to be a paid member of a professional association. Also, you want to verify that this is a group of interest. Once you determine this is a group of interest, click the join this group link.

LinkedIn offers flexibility on how you participate in, manage, and view groups. LinkedIn is a professional social networking site and attracts a lot of people. When you add content to a "group" site, your name is attached to that entry. You can participate in a discussion, but the comments must be relevant, be well written (proper English and spelling), and exhibit knowledge. You need to protect your professional online brand and image. So, proceed with caution!

☐ Attend at Least Four Networking Events

The more people you know, the more opportunities will come your way. Networking isn't all about receiving help; it is giving help as well. It is a give-and-receive relationship with the people you meet. When people think of the word "networking," it is synonymous with "I need a job." Networking isn't about "schmoozing" people, because eventually you will ask for a job. It is more than that. It is a relationship where similar interests are shared. Someone you met could write an e-mail suggesting a local conference with which you are unfamiliar. This is what networking is about: an exchange of information. Please review the Keys to Successfully Working a Networking Event in Box 4.3.

Many of the activities suggested for you to complete each year can be dual purpose. You are probably thinking, attend four events! Where do I get the time? As networking does not come naturally to many people, a goal of collecting "three or four" business cards helps the process. The following events are good opportunities to exchange business cards:

- Career fairs
- Professional association meetings
- Conferences (usually a reduced rate for students)
- Campus clubs
- On-campus lecture series, or
- Concerts or sporting events.

You will have added all the people you know to your LinkedIn account. Now is the time to create an external network. These are people you don't know and want to know. Attending events within your career interests introduces you to a network of people who have similar interests. This is a group of people that you will see often. They are able to assist you in ways unknown to you at this time. You assist them as well. It is a symbiotic relationship.

Mastering the art of small talk is important and is a skill that can be learned. Walking up to people you don't know at events is scary because you think you have nothing to say. You don't know these people! In many ways, it is all about SELF-CONFIDENCE. The confidence to know you can go up to anyone, start a conversation, and keep it going. And, now you have the tool kit to do this. (Note: A helpful tip is to read the newspaper prior to attending an event. You can always chat about the headlines.)

The handshake is followed by the elevator speech. Regardless of the event or location, good body language, a friendly handshake, followed by, "Hi, I'm Jane Smith. I'm a third year student attending the university. And you are?" is all you need to start a conversation. Follow this with being you, being sincere, and saying something general. You could prepare something to say next; however, it is best to keep it spontaneous, as the situation and environment usually assist in providing a topic to discuss.

When you meet someone for the first time, think how Barbara Walters would conduct an interview. Barbara Walters interviews people extremely well and is a good role model. She shows interest in the other person by projecting friendly body language, listening to what the person is saying, encouraging others to talk about themselves, and being honest and sincere. If you ask people questions about themselves, then you sound interested and don't have to talk. Or, keep talking until you find something you have in common with the person. Once you have something in common, the conversation flows naturally. Keep practicing this skill until it comes naturally. (Remember to ask for a business card and give them yours. Keep in touch via LinkedIn.)

BOX 4.3   KEYS TO SUCCESSFULLY WORKING A NETWORKING EVENT

1. **Business cards**—Business cards only cost a few dollars. Business cards with interesting things on them are often kept longer than plain cards. Make sure you have them.
2. **Dress appropriately**—Better to overdress than to underdress. Business attire for men means sport jacket, slacks and a tie, or a business suit. For woman, a business suit or nice slacks with a nice top. Don't dress for the nightclub. Plunging necklines, excessive jewelry, and six-inch heels don't work.
3. **Dress details**—People won't notice if your suit cost $200 or $2,000. But people will notice spaghetti stains on your tie, unpolished shoes, and clothes that don't fit well.
4. **Get to the event early**—Plan on being one of the first ones to the event, and one of the last ones to leave. It's easier to mingle when the crowd is smaller.
5. **Oral hygiene**—On the day of the event, skip the garlic linguine and if possible brush your teeth before the event and carry mints. Check quickly before the event for those green vegetables stuck between the teeth.
6. **Watch the appetizers**—Don't talk with your mouth full of food and don't use your fingers to pick up greasy or saucy snacks. Carry a napkin in your pocket to wipe your fingers if needed. You need to keep one hand free to shake hands with the people you meet.
7. **Avoid walls and corners**—Don't stand with your back to the wall or in a corner. It looks like you're avoiding people. Get into the middle of the room and mix with people.
8. **Elevator speech**—Have a solid elevator speech ready when someone asks, "Tell me about yourself?' or "What do you do?"
9. **Butt in**—You can't talk to the walls. Find someone to talk to, approach that person (or group), and introduce yourself. When approaching a group, don't slink up. Announce your presence. (Also, better to jump into a group than to pick out someone who is by themselves.)
10. **Handshake**—Practice your handshake. Don't be a bone crusher or a jelly fish. Be firm and confident. If you have sweaty palms, carry a paper towel in your pocket and wipe your hand before shaking.
11. **Ask questions**—Don't do all of the talking. Ask open-ended questions and get the other people to talk. Listen to what others have to say so you can ask questions relevant to their story. It's a conversation. Build rapport through common experiences but don't try to "one-up" the other person.
12. **Your body language**—You are being judged by your body language. Don't slouch or cross your arms over your chest. Hold your drink at your side, not in front of your chest. Smile, smile, smile. Use your hands when speaking. Touch people appropriately (touching is okay). Look people in the eyes, but don't stare.

13. **Other people's body language**—Keep your eyes on other people's body language. It will tell you the conversation is finished, long before the person actually says as much. Don't monopolize someone the entire evening.
14. **Be inclusive**—If you are talking to someone and someone else approaches, invite that person into your circle. Introduce people you already know or have met.
15. **Use names**—Once you've been introduced, try to include the other person's name in the conversation, and definitely use that person's name when you say "Nice meeting you" to move on to your next contact.
16. **Quantity vs. quality**—Effective networking means gaining rapport with people. You are better off to come away with three or four solid contacts, than to run around the room collecting 20 business cards.
17. **Follow up**—E-mail everyone you meet. Express your appreciation at spending time with them, offer to help as you can, and let them know how they can help you. If you can remember something about your conversation, mention that in your "nice meeting you" e-mail.
18. **Work as a team**—If you know someone else attending the event, consider working as a team. You head off in one direction, the other person heads off in another direction. When you meet someone, after a few minutes, say "There's someone here I really think you should meet." Then take that person to your associate and hand him or her off. You can pick up a conversation with the person your associate was talking with, or head off to find another prospect.
19. **Don't take it personally**—A lot of very bad networkers go to networking events. Some will ignore you. Some will act condescendingly. Some will look over your shoulder scouting the room while you are talking. Some will try to do all of the talking, and not listen to anything you say. Some will challenge you with controversial statements. Don't take any of it personally. If the conversation is not going well, excuse yourself and find someone else to talk to.
20. **Give up the need to be right**—This is a networking event, not a college debate. Many people will say things with which you disagree, or even that you know to be factually incorrect. Don't correct inconsequential misstatements and don't argue about opinions. Rather, if someone holds an opinion with which you disagree, use it as an opportunity to ask questions and to find out more about that person.

Source: Used with permission from Professor Michael Manahan.

☐ Complete Two Informational Interviews

Targeting a company of interest is one job seeker's strategy. If you attended a career fair, are interested in a specific company, and were adept at obtaining a hiring manager's name, then request an informational interview.

You need to do a search on the person's name and company for title and relevant information if you did not obtain that information. You can use the Internet or your social network to see if anyone has a connection. Call the person and introduce yourself. State that you are interested in the company after attending a job fair, and would like to meet for an informational interview.

Follow up with an e-mail. The interview is a favor to you, so let the person know you will keep it short. When you are conducting an informational interview, the questions are prepared ahead of time. It is important to let the person know what you would like to discuss; you have a purpose. There is a reason you contacted them, want to know them, and seek "inside" information about the company. (There is a difference between information obtained on the Internet about a company and from someone working for the company.)

Before you begin an informational interview, it is a good practice to ask the person how much time he or she has to speak with you. You want to respect the time limit, as people are busy. This informational interview is different from the one suggested in previous chapters. You are requesting an interview from someone who works for a company of interest. You want to know more about the company from the person's perspective. Once again, start off an interview with good body language, a handshake, and your elevator speech. Begin with polite conversation and small talk. Then, start talking about the company; you want to display your knowledge and preparation for the interview. Some questions to ask during an informational interview include the following:

1. What is the culture of the company? How is that exhibited?
2. What are your job responsibilities and duties?
3. What is your background, and education? Do you have special certifications?
4. What professional associations do you belong to?
5. What is your vision for the future of the company?

Discuss the job you are interested in obtaining. Discuss what you have done and propose to do. Ask what more you can do to improve your chances at obtaining that job.

Don't dominate the conversation. You want the person you are interviewing to talk more than you. You show interest in the conversation by taking notes and asking relevant follow-up questions. Know your material, have knowledge of the company, and be yourself! Come prepared with a copy of your résumé, cover letter, and business card. You could request the person to review your résumé and cover letter and offer recommendations. Give the individual your business card and request a business card.

After the interview, follow up with a thank-you e-mail. Be respectful and professional.

EXPERIENCE AND EMPLOYMENT

☐ **Research Companies of Interest**

This is the time to research the companies you want to work for. There is that dream to work for Disney or Google. What would it be like? The first step is to know something about the company. When you begin to research the company, you learn about the type of jobs the company has to offer. You will get a sense if this company is the right fit for you and your qualifications.

Researching a company of interest becomes more important when you start interviewing. It is important to have knowledge about the company in an interview, as it demonstrates initiative, interest, and passion. Preparation prior to an interview separates you from other candidates for the same position.

Where do you find information about various companies?

1. *Visit the company website.* Be sure to know, for example, the correct name of the company. When reviewing the company website, look beneath the home page. Really read the information that is on the web pages. Usually, you can get a sense of the "culture" of the company. It is a formal or informal environment. What is the mission statement? What does that say about the company? Do they have a values statement?

2. *Know the company structure.* Know the names of the CEO and those who report to him or her. Is the company for profit or nonprofit? Is the company privately owned or publicly traded?

3. *Use social media.* One benefit of social media is to ask your network if anyone works for or knows someone who works for the company you are researching. Then, ask that person for an informational interview. There is value in speaking to someone who works for the company. He or she can tell you what the culture of the company is like and what it is like to work for the company each day. Does the company provide training? Does the company offer benefits? These are all good questions to ask on an informational interview.

4. *Look inside the company.* A great website to review employee ratings of a company is *glassdoor.com*. This website has information on various companies by the employees. Just keep in mind that the reviews are by

employees. If an employee "feels" that he or she is treated fairly, then a good review is posted. The opposite is usually true, too.

5. *Conduct an Internet search.* Is there current news regarding the company? If it is a retail company, are new stores opening? Is a new product being released? What is being said regarding the leadership and management of the company?

6. *Find the status in the industry.* Know the company's share in the market, if the company is publicly traded. Know the company's sales and number of employees. Is the company national or international?

7. *Visit the company retail stores if available.* What is the atmosphere of the store; is it friendly? You can tell a lot about a company and products by visiting retail stores.

☐ Obtain an Internship, Summer Employment, Part-Time Employment, or Volunteer in Career Field of Interest

Internships offer a key way to network, learn more about an industry, and enhance your résumé. There are all types of internships. Some internships pay, and some do not.

Possibility of Employment

A paid or unpaid internship offers many benefits. Many of my students obtained permanent jobs upon completing an internship. Why is this possible? Organizational leaders like the enthusiasm students bring to the work environment. As an intern, you are supporting full-time employees. The employees depend on a paycheck and want to perform. The intern who produces for an employee does make an impression. The combination of a good work ethic and a great personality sets the student up for potentially being considered for a full-time position.

Hiring managers would rather hire a potential job applicant they know than go through the interview process to hire an unknown applicant. Interns are in a great position within an organization if a job opening becomes available.

Expand Your Professional Network

As an intern, you meet many people at all levels of the organization. Executives are proud of their internship programs; so you meet the individuals who run the company. Managers distribute the work and recognize good employees.

As stated previously, you will assist full-time employees. Don't forget other interns, too. So, there are many contacts for you. Your job, as an intern, is to network and network extensively. These are the people in your chosen field, and people know other people. If this organization does not have a current job opening, someone in the organization may know of a job position in another company.

The people you meet through your internship are contacts to add to LinkedIn. When you feel comfortable to request a business card from your contacts, send a LinkedIn request. Advance notice to your contacts that you will be sending a LinkedIn request to keep in touch is professional and appreciated. Keep in touch with these people even if a job opportunity is not available presently; there could be job openings in the future. Touch base frequently; at least on a yearly basis.

Display an Excellent Work Ethic and Energetic Personality

The work required of an intern varies depending on the organization and program. You could start out at a position just filing papers or entering data. That can change once you demonstrate your work ethic and social skills. Companies do not want to overwhelm interns because the position is short term. But if you produce, the likelihood of getting better tasks increases. If you do those tasks well, you'll receive more opportunities.

The opposite is true as well. If you don't produce, the tasks you are assigned will be insignificant until your internship ends. It is crucial to take an internship seriously. Look for opportunities where you can contribute; offer ideas. Attend social events when invited. Regardless of the duration of the internship, act like a regular employee.

Learn as Much as Possible

Another benefit of internships is being exposed to a potential career environment. You are in a setting where the people you interact with have the same passions and interests. You have the opportunity to experience the day-to-day routine and atmosphere of a career setting. You are exposed to the language, processes, and procedures of the career. This can be a positive experience or can be a "wake-up call." Yes, you do like the environment and want to continue in pursuit of this career choice, or no, this career choice is not for you.

Summer employment, part-time employment, or volunteer positions offer opportunities to gain experience. So, if an internship is not possible, then seek out other avenues to obtain experience in your field of interest.

Check It Off!

Review the third year in college checklist. How many activities are you able to Check Off?

☐ Update the Work Plan
☐ Assess Job Skills in Related Field of Interest
☐ Obtain Academic Advising
☐ Explore Graduate School
☐ Meet a Career Counselor
☐ Create a Personal Brand
☐ Attend Career Fairs
☐ Attain Leadership Role with Campus Clubs
☐ Attend Professional Association Meetings
☐ Join Toastmasters
☐ Prepare a Job Packet
☐ Obtain Letters of Recommendation
☐ Keep Outstanding Work
☐ Seek Awards and Scholarship Opportunities
☐ Maintain Your LinkedIn Account
☐ Attend at Least Four Networking Events
☐ Complete an Informational Interview
☐ Research Companies of Interest
☐ Obtain an Internship, Summer Employment, Part-Time Employment, or Volunteer in a Career Field of Interest

Chapter Five

Fourth Year in College

"I can't go back to yesterday, because I was a different person then."

—Lewis Carroll, *Alice's Adventures in Wonderland*

The fourth year in college is the transition period from college to career. It is the year to construct a successful job search campaign and obtain employment in your chosen field or finalize plans for graduate school.

OVERVIEW

This is the year you are graduating from college and engaging in commencement activities. *Webster's Dictionary* offers the following definitions of these terms:

- Graduation: the act of receiving a diploma or degree from a school, college, or university, and
- Commencement: to have or mark a beginning.

Change is about to occur, and you are prepared for this change because you completed most, if not all, of the tasks in the previous chapters. Every type of change sets off an emotional chain of events called a transition period. Leaving the known to venture into the unknown is an emotional time for many. *Everyone manages transition in his or her own way and time.* Transition is personal and individualistic. However, the process for everyone is the same: ending, exploration, and new beginning. In your case, it is graduation, "the job search campaign," and commencement.

The bad news: You must deal with the emotions that are surrounding graduating and leaving college, friends, and professors ... familiarity. You are venturing into a new beginning by choosing a career and seeking employment. This is the unknown.

Fourth Year College Checklist

Work Plan and Skill Assessment	☐ Update the Work Plan ☐ Make Use of the Internet ☐ Conduct a Self-Assessment
Academic Advising	☐ Obtain Academic Advising
Career Support	☐ Meet With a Career Counselor ☐ Research the On-Campus Interview Program ☐ **Work** Career Fairs
Academic Clubs and Professional Associations	☐ **Work** the Club Leadership Role ☐ **Work** Professional Association Meetings
Portfolio	☐ Update Portfolio ☐ Perfect Interviewing Skills
Networking	☐ Use LinkedIn ☐ Work Networking Events ☐ Continue Informational Interviews
Experience and Employment	☐ Engage in the Job Search Campaign ☐ Obtain an Internship, Summer Employment, Part-Time Employment, or Volunteer in Career Field of Interest

The good news: YOU ARE PREPARED. You should feel comfortable with the job search campaign because you have the tools and techniques for the undertaking. This is what you worked for in years one through three.

You have the tools and techniques for the job search. In year four, it is about the process. How do you find a job? The answer follows.

WORK PLAN AND SKILL ASSESSMENT

☐ Update the Work Plan

The work plan is more important for the job search campaign. You will be scheduling many tasks that were not done before. For example, you will be sending cover letters and résumés in response to job advertisements. Each company must be documented on the work plan, so you can schedule a follow-up call in two weeks. Keep track of everything, as you will be sending multiple job applications, scheduling and attending events, scheduling and meeting people, and attending workshops and career fairs.

The work plan helps you remember when you applied for jobs and when you need to follow up. The work plan helps you set and review goals. Have I sent eight job packets out this week? After a month or two of keeping an up-to-date work plan, you can assess where you are spending most of your time. If after using the work plan for two months, you have not received one interview request, then it is time to evaluate your job search campaign strategy. Perhaps you will find that you are spending a lot of time on sending job applications and not enough time attending networking events. The work plan is an ideal tool to assist in managing and modifying the job search campaign to get the results you want.

The work plan is changed slightly for the job search campaign (refer to Table 5.1). The headings for the work plan are Date, Task, Job Title, Company, Contact Name and Information, Website, Status, and Additional Information. Status and Additional Information columns are kept to help you keep track of activities. Of course, you can add more headings to the Excel worksheet to facilitate your campaign. These column headings are to assist in logging the activities associated with the job search campaign.

You need to log the jobs applied for. Include all pertinent information such as whether you were called for an interview, when you interviewed, and contacts with whom you may want to meet. (Note: There is free software other than using an Excel worksheet that is available on the Internet. Search for the tool that best serves your purpose for the job search.)

The job search campaign is a proactive rather than reactive approach. You look for job advertisements and apply to them. Many times, you will not hear back from a company: you didn't make the cut, the job opening was canceled, the company hired a "known" individual, or the company changed the job requirement. The proactive task is to follow up if possible and keep at the process of looking for employment until you reach your goal. Keeping records of the jobs applied for and the people you meet will facilitate the proactive rather than reactive approach to the job search.

☐ Make Use of the Internet

From setting up your e-mail to searching online databases for job advertisements, the Internet is a necessity for the job search. You must be comfortable using the Internet and searching online databases using keywords efficiently. While the Internet is a top resource in finding employment, there is more to a job search than using a computer. You must make a point to get away from the computer, too!

Table 5.1. Work Plan for the Job Search Campaign

Date	Task	Job Title	Company	Contact Name and Information	Website	Status	Additional Information
01/10/16	Send job packet to Peters/job ad on peters. com database	Entry-Level Accountant	The Peters Company	John Smith 112 Burbank Road Burbank, CA 91307 jsmith@peters.com	peters.com	Sent. Waiting for response and will follow up in two weeks	
02/15/16	Send job packet to Jones Accounting/job ad on jones.com database	Junior Accountant	Jones and Company	Judy Jones 566 Grand Street Glendale, CA 97789	jones.com	Sent. Received reply on 3/1/16	Phone interview scheduled for 3/10/2016
03/15/16	Attend Accounting Professional Function			Marriott Hotel Crystal Room 444 Hyatt Parkway Glendale, CA 97789			Want to meet Sarah Smith, Director of Accounting at Walsmith Want to meet John Ohr, Manager of Accounting at Colorstore

Many websites are available that can assist with developing your toolkit: the résumé, cover letter, elevator speech, business cards, and interview skills. It is a good idea to review those sites and take advantage of what they have to offer. Also, creating résumé statements or cover letters doesn't have to be 100% original. Take advantage of sample résumés and cover letters posted on the Internet to extract and modify the information that fits your profile.

Another resource that seems antiquated (but isn't) and often overlooked is the public library. The public library may be able to help if you are not comfortable using the Internet. You can learn basic computer skills necessary to navigate the Internet and assist in every stage of the job search.

The public library is rich in resources, from professional librarians who can assist with the job search to the computer stations available for free. Public libraries offer free classes, workshops, and basic job search services. Plus, the books are available for free: books on how to write a résumé and cover letter with examples (make sure you use recent books, however). Find out what your library, what the school library, and neighboring community libraries have to offer. You'll be surprised.

☐ Conduct a Self-Assessment

During year one, you (1) completed self-assessments and met with a career counselor to review the outcomes. In year two, you (2) analyzed the trend in the job market over the next five to ten years. In years one, two, and three, you (3) acquired experience in your chosen career field by working full- or part-time, obtaining internships, or doing volunteer work.

Prior to engaging in the job search campaign, a thorough self-assessment of the three areas is necessary. The assessment processes will help you to:

- analyze your skill set and what you have to offer,
- target your desired job by knowing specific job titles, and
- provide information on areas needed for improvement and training.

Potential employers look for the following work proficiencies: skills, knowledge, experience, accomplishments, and personality traits. It is critical that you are able to demonstrate positive character traits through statements about past experience.

The question that needs answering is this: Do you have the skills, knowledge, experience, accomplishments, and personality traits based upon what you have accomplished during the previous three years? How prepared are you to start responding to job advertisements and begin the interview process? Now is the time to analyze your skill set through education and experience targeted to the specific job title you are seeking. Is more training or experience needed prior to the job search campaign, or are you ready to begin?

ACADEMIC ADVISING

☐ **Obtain Academic Advising**

Prior to the fourth year, most students declare a major and are assigned an academic advisor affiliated with the major department or program. The advisor meets with the student to assist in planning the major, identify research opportunities, and discuss postgraduate opportunities in the field. You need to meet often with the academic advisor to discuss your overall progress toward the degree, plus support postgraduation.

Most faculty have a network of colleagues both inside and outside of the academic field and have connections with people who work in various companies within your field of interest. Another source of support in finding a position upon graduation is to discuss opportunities with your major advisor. If your GPA is above average, and you have a relationship with your major advisor, there are many opportunities available where the advisor could help. Take the time to schedule appointments, have your questions ready, and discuss opportunities with your advisor.

CAREER SUPPORT

☐ **Meet with a Career Counselor**

Meet with the career counselor this year to:

- critique your résumé and cover letter,
- provide instruction on interview preparation,
- provide opportunities to practice interviewing,
- obtain information on how to dress for job fairs and interviews,
- obtain information regarding the on-campus interview program,
- prepare for career fairs,
- seek assistance in using the Career Center job employment database, and
- prepare for graduate schools (if interested).

The Career Center exists to assist students by providing career workshops, special events, and job search strategies. The career counselor is the person to support you through job search preparation and strategy. If you took the advice in the previous years to develop a relationship with a specific career counselor, this is the year where that relationship is helpful. Take advantage of the services and opportunities the center offers.

☐ Research the On-Campus Interview Program

Most colleges and universities offer an On-Campus Interview Program. The college, usually hosted by the Career Center, invites employers to campus to interview graduating students for full-time career positions. Employer participants include business, industry, nonprofit organizations, and government agencies. Positions are generally entry level in nature and encompass a broad range of functional areas, including, but not limited to, finance, marketing, management, sales, operations, social service, technology, engineering, and laboratories. The program is "free" to students, as you pay for it through your tuition or student service charges.

The interview is a one-on-one interview, one student per employer. It is an excellent service provided by the college. Check with your college or university to verify if a program does exist and the requirements you must meet. Most often, this program is available to alumni as well.

☐ Work Career Fairs

You are familiar with attending job fairs hosted by your college or university. Now is the time to take the opportunity to "work" the fair for the job search. First, contact the Career Center in advance of the fair to find out which companies will be participating. Select those companies that you want to meet and take the time to do research regarding the company, before the fair.

When at the fair, have your elevator speech prepared along with a copy of a cover letter, résumé, and business card. Dress professionally as you would on an interview (review the interview section).

The company employees working the fair are not the hiring managers but the human resource professionals. Once eye contact is made, you need to be self-confident, assured, and prepared. You shake hands and deliver your elevator speech. Be very specific on the type of position you are seeking. You come prepared with questions. For example, "What is your company's statistic on hiring new graduates?" You state, "I have a copy of a cover letter and résumé that I would like to give you. What is the process after receiving this information?" If you have additional questions, be prepared to ask.

Your ability to make an impression is limited to approximately five minutes. So, you must practice your introduction, delivery, and questions prior to attending the job fair. Don't try and "wing it."

Once the conversation has reached a natural conclusion, obtain contact information for this particular person or the hiring manager and state that YOU will follow up after the fair. Make notes after the conversation so that you have the information when writing a follow-up email. The e-mail should be sent within two days from the fair.

Two websites that provide information regarding job fairs are:

1. www.collegegrad.com/jobsearch/job-fair-success
2. www.quintcareers.com/career_fair_tutorial

ACADEMIC CLUBS AND PROFESSIONAL ORGANIZATIONS

☐ Work the Club Leadership Role

If you are successful in obtaining a club leadership role, you can use this role to your advantage. For example, if you haven't given many presentations in your career and would like to add this skill to your portfolio, now is the time to schedule such an event. Talk to the club executive team, propose a topic to present based upon an interest, and schedule the event to occur.

If you need more leadership experience, then volunteer to coordinate an event where you will schedule a speaker to come and present at one of the meetings. This is the time to review your résumé and assess what skills are missing or need enhancement. Then, take it upon yourself to formulate and execute an idea to add that skill set to your résumé. Also, you can add the presentation or other document prepared for the event to your portfolio.

You can take these opportunities to another level; write an article on the topic or event and submit to your college newspaper or post on your on-line club page. Most student clubs are happy to have people volunteer their time, effort, and especially ideas to make the club a better experience for all. Once again, this is another entry on your résumé.

The ideas presented do not add that much time to an already busy schedule and enhance your résumé considerably. Look for opportunities to enhance your résumé and portfolio where they are lacking.

☐ Work Professional Association Meetings

If you have researched and joined a professional association affiliated with your major, once again, this is the time to take advantage of what the group offers and what you can offer the group.

Discussion on networking with individuals and employers in the industry through participating and attending professional association meetings must be reiterated. Now is the time to meet at least five people at each association meeting, provide the members with your business cards, and state that you are looking for employment after college graduation. You should be specific in the type of job you are interested in pursuing. You are not asking for a job; you are letting people know you are seeking employment.

Highlighting your membership on your résumé indicates to employers the dedication to your career. If you have volunteered to work on a function for the association, highlight these activities on the résumé, too.

As with the "club leadership role" advice, here too is a chance to take advantage of student leadership opportunities. If you need to add a specific skill set to your résumé, volunteer to gain experience in that targeted area. If you need leadership, management, marketing, accounting, or business experience, professional associations offer opportunities to enhance that skill set with little to no negative consequences. Usually, students are more abreast on current information and topics within their major than professionals, as students are learning this information in their classes. Offering to present at a professional organizational meeting on current trends within the field is an idea that adds to your credibility within the field. This one act demonstrates confidence, self-assurance, and knowledge in the field.

Also, professional associations put on conferences and conventions providing members with access to exclusive career resources, such as job postings, information about seminars, publications, or training and certification courses that may be suitable for your vocational path.

PORTFOLIO

Refer to Table 2.2.

☐ **Update Portfolio**

Job Packet

It is important to update your portfolio when you begin the job search campaign. The Career Center offers workshops on résumé, cover letter, and stellar reference preparation. Take the workshops and update the job packet. Give the cover letter and résumé to the Career Center counselor to critique. If you know someone in your career field, provide the individual with your cover letter and résumé and ask for a professional critique. People want to help, so reach out. If you do not know someone in your field, use your social networking site, LinkedIn, to connect with someone.

The résumé's purpose is to motivate an employer to interview you. It should target your abilities and background relevant to the job desired. Write one résumé per job application. Verify that the keywords from the job description are emphasized within the résumé. Focus on accomplishments at work and not just responsibilities. Remember to coordinate the résumé to the LinkedIn profile.

The cover letter is not the résumé. The cover letter describes accomplishments that cannot be explained fully within the résumé. You want to include the keywords from the job description in the cover letter.

Update your stellar reference list and verify that the contact information is correct. Let your stellar references know that you are starting the job search and you will notify them when you receive an interview request.

Verify that the information on your business cards is correct and that you have an ample supply.

Keep in mind the importance of marketing or branding yourself. All documents must have the same look—same font type and style. Verify that your résumé is the same as your LinkedIn account. The job packet must look professional; use proper English, without spelling or grammatical errors.

Letters of Recommendation, Examples of Work, Awards, and Scholarships

Continue to seek letters of recommendation, and award and scholarship opportunities in the fourth year of college. As a fourth-year student, you are permitted to apply for scholarships. Seek out the scholarships available by discussing opportunities with the Career Center and the academic advisor. You can discuss opportunities available with the department chair in your area of interest.

Place yourself in a position to seek awards by leading clubs and activities. If awards are not part of the particular club you attend, suggest starting this activity at an end-of-the-year get-together.

Prior to Your First Interview

Update the portfolio to bring to an interview. Review the letters of recommendation, examples of your work, and awards and scholarships kept from years one through four. Select the best papers to highlight your skills: writing, presentation, computer, and the like. If there is one particular project that you are proud of doing, include that in your portfolio as well. Quality is better than quantity.

Place the portfolio information in an organized binder, with separators, in preparation for the job interview. On an interview, you want to be able to get the information you need to present to the interviewer quickly and without leafing through the binder.

☐ Perfect Interviewing Skills

The résumé gets you an interview; the interview gets you the job! It seems many students are leery about the interview process. To calm nerves, preparation is the key; you cannot "wing it." Companies do not interview everyone who applies for a position. If your skills and abilities match the job description, you are in a better position to be asked to interview. During the interview, the interviewer is determining the best "fit" for the position; the interviewer is evaluating your personality and knowledge.

Many books are written on the interview process. They offer information on the types of interviews, answers to tough questions, the things to say to get you the job you want, and what to wear and not to wear at the interview. Also, the Internet provides a lot of information for free on the interview process. (Refer to Appendix E: Interview Preparation for more information.)

Before the Interview: Preparation

1. Organize your portfolio. Place several copies of the cover letter, résumé, and stellar references for the position for which you are interviewing into the binder. Include several business cards.
2. Review the job description for which you are interviewing. Make notes on the keywords listed in the job description. You want to use these words during the interview.
3. Research the company prior to going on the interview. Use the Internet, visit the company, and visit the company stores. Know the leaders, company products, finances, goals, competition, accomplishments, and the like. Also, check the news; you need to know what is current.
4. If you know someone who works for the company, ask that person out for coffee. State that you have an interview with the company and you would like some information about the company from the employee's perspective. Conduct an informational interview.
5. Prepare six to eight questions to ask the interviewer about the company when asked. Usually the last question in an interview is, "Do you have any questions for me?" You should have prepared questions. Asking questions exhibits knowledge and interest.
6. Practice answering the basic interview questions. The first question in most interviews is, "Tell me about yourself?" The answer is your elevator

speech. The Career Center offers interview skills workshops; also, you can use software or your smartphone to record answering questions for practice. When you playback the video, errors in interviewing are recognized and easily corrected.

7. When called for an interview, ask what the dress code is for the interview. It could be that wearing a Hawaiian shirt to an interview for Trader Joe's is a better idea than showing up wearing a suit and tie. This indicates to the interviewer that you did your research on the company.

Day of the Interview: Before the Interview

1. Arrive on time, not too early and especially not late. If you are going to be late, please call to let them know and give the reason. People understand.
2. Dress appropriately as discussed previously. Check yourself in the mirror prior to the interview. (Showing what you had for lunch is not attractive. As an interviewer, this has happened more than once while interviewing a candidate. It is difficult to focus.) Avoid perfume, excess makeup, or large jewelry. Keep your dress style conservative. Have fresh breath; this is imperative for those who smoke.
3. Greet the receptionist and provide small talk. Receptionists are the most knowledgeable people in the company about relationships. You can talk about the traffic or weather. You can complement the receptionist on his or her clothing. You want to be personable and exhibit a personality. You want this person to like you.

Day of the Interview: During the Interview

1. On the walk from the reception area to the interview room, make small talk. The purpose of an interview is to demonstrate your personality People do the hiring, not organizations.
2. Once in the interview room, present a hard copy of your cover letter, résumé, and stellar reference list to each interviewer. Shake hands with all interviewers prior to sitting.
3. Answer questions completely and succinctly using proper English. If you don't understand the question, ask for the question to be restated. Don't answer a question you don't understand. Just state, "Can you please rephrase the question, as I'm not sure what you are asking?" Or, state "By _____, do you mean _____?"
4. When answering questions:
   a. Remember to use the keywords. You want the interviewer to know that you are qualified for the position.

b. Express your knowledge about the company. It is important that you let the interviewer know that you did your research.

c. Use your portfolio. Present the information in your portfolio at appropriate times when answering questions. For example, if the question is, "What would your peers say about your work ethic?" this would be the time to present your letters of recommendation. Use the information in your portfolio as examples to answer questions related to your work.

d. Answer questions by relating a story. People remember stories better than facts. For example, if the question is, "Tell me about a time when you were in a leadership position?" You could relate a story about organizing an outdoor fund-raiser. The day before the event you checked the weather forecast and there was an 80–90% chance of rain. You explain how you were able to recruit all volunteers to relocate the event to an inside venue, create signs and banners, and communicate effectively through social media this change in location.

5. Take notes. Even if you are not a good notetaker, open up a notepad and scribble something. Note takers are perceived as more engaged and attentive.

6. Print out information from the company's website and highlight sections liberally. When asked "what do you know about our company" pull out your highlighted sheets and flip through them (making sure the interviewer can see the printouts and your highlights). The interviewer will be impressed with your preparedness.

7. Find a balance between listening and speaking. In fact, a good rule is to listen 55% during the interview and speak only 45%. Good interviews are those where the interviewer speaks 90% of the time! Always keep your answers brief and to the point.

8. Ask your list of prepared questions at convenient points throughout the interview. Unanswered questions are asked at the end of the interview. *Do not ask about benefits or salary.* Those discussions take place once you obtain a job offer.

9. Toward the end of the interview, express your interest in the position. If you are interested in an offer of employment, state that fact. Very few people ask for the position at the time of the interview. This is not a time to be shy. If you want the position, ask for the position.

10. Ask what happens next. You want to know what the next stages in the employment process are and when they may occur. You state that you will call (preferably) or e-mail in two weeks to follow up on the position. Verify that you have the correct contact information before leaving the interview.

11. At the end of the interview, thank the interviewer for his or her time and shake hands. On the walk from the interview room to the reception area, once again make small talk. Say good-bye to the receptionist.

After the Interview

1. Take a few minutes after the interview to note impressions and feelings regarding the experience. Note your positive and negative feelings about the company, interview, and the like. How would you critique yourself? What questions did you have trouble answering? What would you have done differently?
2. Send a thank you letter (or e-mail) to the interviewer(s) reiterating your interest in the position.
3. Make a note in your work plan that you will follow up in two weeks if you have not heard from the hiring manager. Be proactive.

NETWORKING

☐ **Use LinkedIn**

LinkedIn can be used as an effective job search tool for job seekers. It includes a job database, profiles of thousands of recruiters and hiring managers, and detailed company information, to name a few.

Prior to using LinkedIn for the job search, you need to update your profile and maintain your network of connections. Remember to include the keywords relevant to your area of interest. Complete your online résumé and indicate on your profile that you are seeking employment. Recruiters, human resource professionals, and hiring managers view LinkedIn for potential employee candidates.

LinkedIn offers a database of job postings. To search for a job posting, you must enter search criteria such as keywords, job titles, or company names. LinkedIn has advanced job search techniques if you have specific criteria for a search. The job postings will be displayed based on the specific criteria entered. The content on a job posting varies dependent upon what the hiring company chooses to enter or display to the job seeker. The information displayed is interactive, meaning you can communicate to the person who posted the job advertisement. This varies dependent on the hiring company.

LinkedIn offers several ways to apply for jobs, based on the way the company posting the job handles recruitment. You can apply for a job posted on LinkedIn directly from a job posting or link to a company's website to apply for the position.

Learn the system and use it to your advantage when seeking employment.

☐ Work Networking Events

The two types of events professionals usually attend are related to work: conferences and professional association meetings. These events are dual purposed. First is to gain information or learn something new. Usually, an educational component is attached to conferences or professional associations. Second is networking. This is a get-together where you meet people in the same field and have the same work interest.

With either event, most attendees are not quick to pass on their résumé to anyone with the hope of getting some feedback. Attendees will meet, greet, and hand out business cards. After the event, the attendee will follow up and discuss employment opportunities.

As a note, conferences usually incorporate an area for résumé posting, job database searches, and employer meetups for those individuals interested in seeking a job. It is important to take advantage of these opportunities.

However, networking events, as stated in previous chapters, should be viewed as get-togethers unrelated to work as well. This list gives a few examples of such activities, which can include any particular function that you attend based on personal interests:

• Social events
• Political fund-raisers
• Sporting events or parties
• Church-sponsored activities
• Fund-raisers
• Social activities such as runs or bike-a-thons, and
• Events for children.

This year, you are to connect with others doing the activities that you enjoy. You come to the event with a goal of introducing yourself to five people and obtaining contact information via business cards or smartphone.

You are in a good position to connect to others because of your shared interest. You attend events and participate in activities that you are most passionate about. These are the activities where you focus your time and effort outside of work. Creating small talk with people with the same interest should be relatively easy. It is up to you to take these opportunities and introduce yourself, and get to know five people during the course of an event.

Over time, continuing these activities will increase your social network tremendously. The line separating our public life from our private life is now blurred. As we have come to understand, networking is about the people you know, who know other people who may have a connection to an organization or function you are interested in pursuing. When you redefine the art of "networking" as engaging with other people, sharing activities of interest, and enjoying passions, then it takes the "work" out of networking and becomes an effortless way to expand your social contacts.

☐ Continue Informational Interviews

Informational interviews are more important once the job search begins. The informational interview is one technique to use when you want to meet someone to discuss a company of interest. The informational interview communicates firsthand experiences and impressions of someone in the company and field of choice and is directed by your questions.

During the job search campaign, obtaining knowledge about the company and learning about the company's culture are significant. This information is important when writing a cover letter and when interviewing for a position. The best way to know about a company and its culture is to talk to an employee. This is accomplished using the informational interview technique. (Note: This is not the only way to obtain information about a company; use the other techniques discussed in the preceding chapters.)

"It's what you learn after you think you know it all that counts."

(Coach John Wooden)

During an informational interview, you can discuss how the organization functions on a day-to-day basis and relate it to your own likes and dislikes. Questions can be asked during informational interviews that normally are not discussed during a job interview. For example, is dressing in a suit required each day? How flexible is the vacation policy? What company benefits are offered to employees? Beyond the advantages of gaining valuable career information, the informational interview provides the opportunity to build self-confidence and to improve your ability to handle the job interview.

EXPERIENCE AND EMPLOYMENT

☐ Engage in the Job Search Campaign

This is the area in the book where you take all you have learned during these four years and begin the job search campaign. The mind-set for starting the job search is this: "I am going to get a job, a great job." Keep repeating the phrase, because finding employment is not an overnight endeavor. Finding the right job will take time, dedication, and persistence.

You'll hear many "nos" before you hear the word "yes." But it only takes that one opportunity.

Finding employment is a full-time activity. You need to manage your activities using the work plan. You add tasks and assign dates to those tasks. You set goals for yourself.

Stick to a schedule when looking for employment. For example, work on finding employment four days a week—eight-hour days. Take Fridays off to go to the movies, to play golf, and so on. On Saturday and Sunday, organize your "to do" list for the following week.

The onus on finding employment is on YOU! The phone is not going to ring spontaneously offering you a dream job. What you do is to use the information learned in the four years of college and apply it to finding employment.

The job search campaign consists of active and passive activities.

Active Activities

A. Target companies
- Arrange informational interviews
- Contact your social network

B. Network
- Contact your social network
- Contact stellar references
- Attend professional association meetings
- Attend career fairs
- Contact college alumni office

Passive Activities

C. Research and apply to job advertisements
D. Contact search firms
E. Use social networking sites' databases

A. Target Companies

Do you want to work for a specific company? You may know of a company that has the right culture and environment. You start by defining the list of target companies that interest you. Once done, you must become knowledgeable about the organization and how you would fit within the organization. You must identify the appropriate areas where your skill set is desired. Next, you contact the hiring manager within the organization and specific area. You send a cover letter and résumé stating your interest in the organization and employment opportunities. You finish with stating that you will call in two weeks to follow up on the request and schedule an interview.

You need to be very specific on your fit within the organization. You must become familiar and knowledgeable with the organization before it offers the opportunity to interview. And, you must schedule a follow-up with the hiring manager in two weeks. Do not be discouraged if your first attempts are not successful. Keep trying. Give yourself a couple of months and reach out again. Be persistent but professional.

Contact your social network, people you know, in order to connect to the people—they know who work for the company. Does anyone know of a contact at the company? Once you have a name of a person, schedule an informational interview. The best information comes from the people who work for the company. Let your network WORK for you.

B. Network

Get the word out—you are looking for a job! The best way to get the word out is to use your network. It's the most effective technique of finding work. Many people resist using this technique, as they don't want to bother people. Yet, people want to help other people. Social networking sites such as LinkedIn and Facebook make this an easier task. Social networking sites provide an opportunity to reach individuals whose links you need to connect to a person or job advertisement to facilitate the job search.

When you network, you seek information, advice, ideas, names, and referrals. These contacts lead you to other contacts, who can ultimately lead to a job advertisement or opportunity. The key to remember about networking is that you are not asking for a job. You are marketing yourself, letting people know that you are seeking employment.

Whom do you contact? The following list is a good place to start:

- Adult relatives
- Close friends
- Alumni
- Current or former neighbors
- Dentist, doctor, and the like
- Lawyer, accountant, realtor, and the like
- Religious or social organizations
- Professional association
- Campus clubs
- Colleagues, vendors, suppliers—people you have worked with
- Customers or clients
- Consultants

Contact your stellar references and let them know you are starting the job search. Let your references know that you will inform them of job opportunities and interviews and will keep them abreast of your activities.

Your references will come away with a positive impression and a sense that you are organized and professional.

Attend professional association meetings and announce to the people you meet that you are beginning the job search and hand out your business card. State the type of position that you are interested in pursuing and if a person hears of something, to please let you know. Often professional association meetings have a segment where they match the companies looking for qualified candidates to the employees seeking employment.

Attend career fairs and target those companies that you are interested in working for.

You will soon become an alumnus of the university or college you are attending. It is not too soon to reach out to the alumni office and state that you are seeking employment, as most alumni offices will assist you in seeking employment.

C. Research and Apply to Job Advertisements

With the advent of the Internet, access to job advertisements is available twenty-four hours a day, seven days a week. Once you have access to the Internet, you can access thousands of free resources with job listings. Because there is so much information, the problem is to know where to look. There are two categories of websites: general recruitment and niche job boards. Don't discount either category, but statistics on niche job boards are preferred by recruiters and human resource professionals.

General recruitment These sites draw job postings from numerous online sources:

- CareerBuilder.com
- Monster.com
- LinkedIn.com
- Jobster.com
- Indeed.com
- Simplyhired.com
- Toupusajobs.com
- Linkup.com

Niche job boards These sites are specific to the job area of interest:

- Company sites
- Industry-specific online sites, such as
  www.accounting.com (accounting jobs)
  www.hrcareerusa.com (human resource jobs)
  www.dice.com (technology jobs)

- Professional associations
- Government sites
- Nonprofit sites: idealist.org

Online search tips The use of online databases for job advertisements is a tedious task. You should find helpful the following online search tips.

1. *Know what you are searching for.* You have done a lot of work in years one through four on finding job titles and keywords. These are the words to use in your Internet search.
2. *Set aside several hours a day to search the online job advertisement databases.* Keep setting goals and meeting goals. If your targets are unrealistic, then set new goals. Be your best friend, not your worst enemy.
3. *Set a goal to apply to eight or more (your choice) job advertisements per week.* The length of time you apply and hear back may be longer than you expect. An average wait is three to four weeks. The reason for applying to many job advertisements per week is the wait time; you may not hear back from many employers. So, this is where you begin to get discouraged. You must be patient and realize that job searching requires persistence.
4. *Be diligent regarding maintaining the work plan.* Each job advertisement sent is an entry into the work plan to follow up within two weeks. Many job advertisements have the contact information included. This information must be entered into the work plan to facilitate good management.
5. *Limit the time online to 25% of the total time you dedicate to your job search.* The number of hours spent sitting in front of a computer becomes addictive. Make your time on the computer productive.
6. *Don't share personal information.* Beware of advertisements requesting personal information such as your Social Security number or bank account numbers. Sharing this information is not part of the job search process.

D. Contact Search Firms

Search firms work for employers and are paid by the employers to locate qualified people for specific positions. Also, search firms screen the job candidates prior to scheduling an interview with the employer. There are hundreds of search firms ranging in size from a one-person company to a large international firm.

There are two types of search firms: retainer and contingency.

1. Retainer search firms contract specifically with that company for that position; no other firm is competing with them to fill the position.
2. Contingency search firms contract specifically with that company for that position, but several other firms may be referring candidates.

The process is you contact the search firm by sending it a brief cover letter and a copy of your résumé. You should include the title of the position you are seeking. Additional information that is important is the geographic area of preference and salary requirements.

The search firm enters your information into its database. Your qualifications, based on the cover letter and résumé, are matched against the job advertisements in their respective database. If there is a match, you will be called for an interview.

The search firm's fee is approximately 20–30% the annual starting salary of the employee. With this being said, search firms spend their time on candidates they "feel" will give them a good return on investment. That means recruiters will contact you only if your background and skills are an exact match to the job opening they are trying to fill. However, there are exceptions. If a recruiter has worked with or placed someone you know, then you have a better chance of getting some of the recruiter's time; you may be able to get an interview. Or, perhaps the recruiter is your aunt or uncle!

An important note: As a job seeker, you commit to one recruiter per job opening. It is not permissible to use multiple recruiters for the same job opening.

E. Use Social Networking Sites' Databases

Refer to the Use LinkedIn section for using social networking sites' databases for the job search.

☐ Obtain an Internship, Summer Employment, Part-time Employment, or Volunteer in Career Field of Interest

There are many times when internships, summer employment, or part-time employment turn into full-time employment. So, do not discount the possibility that a small position could escalate into a full-time job.

Getting to know people, attending company events, and socializing with the employees are beneficial if your interests are to obtain full-time employment at the organization you are interning. Of course, you must perform in your job—that goes without saying. But, organizations hire people when the personality of the individual and fit within the organization are a match.

Check It Off!

Review the fourth year in college checklist. How many activities are you able to Check Off?

☐ Update the Work Plan
☐ Conduct a Self-Assessment
☐ Obtain Academic Advising
☐ Meet with a Career Center
☐ Research the On-Campus Interview Program
☐ Work Career Fairs
☐ Work the Club Leadership Role
☐ Work Professional Association Meetings
☐ Update your Portfolio
☐ Perfect Interviewing Skills
☐ Maintain your LinkedIn Account
☐ Work Networking Events
☐ Complete Informational Interviews
☐ Engage in the Job Search Campaign
☐ Obtain an Internship, Summer Employment, Part-Time Employment, or Volunteer in Career Field of Interest

Chapter Six

Wrap It Up

"Every adventure requires a first step!"

—Lewis Carroll, *Alice's Adventures in Wonderland*

The one big mistake many students make in college is to worry about the cost and outcome. Most students spent 80% or more on their time concentrating on completing college because of the cost and 20% or less of the time enjoying the journey. By the time you figure out how to navigate the system, the courses you should take, and the professors to study with, the program is over! Most students state that if they had "a do over," they would take an extra year to savor the experience.

There are not a lot of stories about people and students throughout the book. Every person is different, and everyone's story is different. Everyone's journey is different because of the various factors affecting individual lives. You are responsible for your own journey! It is up to you to seek out the support you need to pursue your career. Have the confidence, yes the CONFIDENCE, to talk to professors, librarians, career counselors, and academic advisors to provide the information you need to pave your way through college to a career! And *enjoy* the journey.

FINAL THOUGHTS

Getting Good Grades

Check It Off! is about the tasks to navigate through college to career, not about grades. However, it is worth mentioning in the summary chapter that good grades open doors to opportunities. For example, if you are competing for scholarships, you need to have good grades: at least a 3.5 GPA (4.0). Most students who apply for scholarships have really good grades. It is a given.

Grades are important when you are in college, to seek opportunities such as internships, and to obtain your first job. Once you are in the workplace, your GPA has less impact unless you apply to graduate school or other academic institutions.

Many prestigious programs screen college candidates by GPA. For example, if you are interested in applying to the FBI, or opportunities in government, your grades are important. Of course, the GPA is not the only criterion used to evaluate your credentials when you apply for a program, but having poor grades automatically eliminates your application. Your grades do not have to be perfect, but they do have to be high enough to be competitive. You are in college to learn, so don't shy away from a class because it is difficult. However, apply yourself and work hard in your courses to get the best possible grade.

Choosing a Career Is Not a Linear Path

Dr. Wayne Dyer (2004) in his book, *The Power of Intention: Learning to Co-Create Your World Your Way*, stated that if you don't have a career goal in mind, then your goal is to find a career. Get over the idea that what you study in college directly relates to a career. Many people working in the information technology field majored in music. Their stories differed on what led them to information technology; however, most of them still performed during the evenings and on weekends. They did not give up on their passion for music.

Changing careers is more the norm than exception. Many people start out in one field and change. Karyn majored in geology because her dad was a geologist. Once she graduated from college, she applied to graduate school for geology. After spending several years in the field, she gave it all up to go back to school to study physical therapy. There are various reasons, many psychological, on why we choose fields or interests to pursue. Regardless of the reasons, eventually you will find the job you were meant to have. Does it take time? For many people, it is a non-linear approach. Few people know their area of interest and pursue one career from high school through to retirement.

If you took the assessment tests in year one, you know a great deal about yourself. The tests and the courses taken should provide some insight on what you like and your interests. If you are still undecided about a career, get a job with exposure to many disciplines, so you can have experience in various fields. After working in various positions for a while, you will determine the one field that you would like to pursue.

Many of the skills learned and courses taken in college prepare you for multiple jobs. Skills such as communication, leadership, management, and computers are applicable to multiple careers. Personality traits are very important; do you work well independently and in a team? Can you demonstrate this with personal stories and experiences gained from college courses? Once you obtain a position with a generic skill set and find the career you want to pursue, then find the courses and classes that will enable you to obtain the skill set for that position. You need to obtain the skills for that position by knowing the keywords, taking classes, and obtaining experience.

Finding a Job Is a Proactive Rather Than Reactive Activity

Finding a job is a proactive rather than a reactive activity. That means you are actively working to find a job at least four to five days a week eight hours a day—rest on the weekends. You are looking for job advertisements, applying to job advertisements, revising your résumé and cover letter, seeking out events to attend, attending events, and networking both in person and through social media. You schedule informational interviews and meet people. You get asked to interview, research prior to the interview, and follow up after an interview. All of these activities are yours to complete. You are not waiting for an e-mail or phone call in any of these activities.

If you are out of work, you can seek work using "temp" agencies, volunteer, or part-time opportunities. When you consider these three options, it doesn't seem to correlate with spending four years in college, working very hard to obtain good grades, to then obtain a "menial" job. There are several benefits to having a basic job when seeking a career opportunity.

First, and foremost, are networking opportunities. You are able to meet people you would not have met sitting at home. These people know other people. So, talk to them whenever you get the chance, or ask people out for coffee. Second, you are learning about the organization. You can observe how the organization is run and what type of jobs you are attracted to. Finally, temporary jobs often lead to full-time positions. If the people you work with like you and respect your work ethic, when a position becomes available you are in a better position for consideration.

A final option is to consider going into business for yourself. Become an entrepreneur. This is actually easier than you might think, at first. Many free programs can help you create your own website. This is helpful in creating your own business. Starting your own business may not be what you want to do long term, but in the short term you develop skills that are transferable to the work place. As an entrepreneur you demonstrate drive, initiative, passion, and perseverance.

The Path to Getting a Great Job Is to Network

You must learn to network all of the time, and as described in previous chapters, networking is not a difficult task. You join, interact, and meet people doing the activities that you enjoy. As you are singing in the choir or attending a concert, you obtain contact information and add the contact to your LinkedIn account. You are meeting and developing a mutually rewarding relationship through networking. One day, you will be called upon by someone you met just as you will call upon that individual for information. Networking is a give-and-take relationship.

Learning how to use small talk and delivering your elevator speech are two important techniques to networking. You will use these techniques throughout your career. What would happen if you meet your boss's boss on an elevator? Do you say nothing until they exit the elevator? Or, you are at the airport and run into the CEO of the company, who by the way recognizes you. Do you say nothing? These two situations are career opportunities that cannot be ignored. With practice, you will learn how to shake hands, introduce yourself, and deliver your elevator speech. Your confidence is evident as you demonstrate professionalism and courtesy.

Books are available on how to talk to anyone and how to network effectively. So, if you are having difficulty or need more information on how to network, it is available. How to make a great first impression, how to convey professionalism through proper body language, how to dress professionally, and how to communicate effectively are important concerns when approaching someone for the first time. Reaching out to people to connect can be an awkward experience. Sometimes people are friendly and react as such and sometimes not. More often than not, you will be successful in the approach. Networking is an important activity to learn and undertake for your career.

Work First, and Then Consider Graduate School

Obtain a couple of years' work experience before considering graduate school. The major reason for this recommendation is that work experience provides exposure to various fields that were not considered during college. It takes time and experience to learn the nuances of an organization and where interests truly lie. You need to take time to settle into your career before you venture out into taking more classes. You may find in working for an organization that you want to learn more about strategic planning or leadership. You may initially think to obtain an MBA, but a better alternative may be an MA in organizational development. These decisions take time to discover and research.

Another reason to work for a couple of years prior to going to graduate school is that you may need the graduate courses to fill gaps in your résumé.

For example, if you are working in a particular field but don't have the experience in a particular area, a graduate school course may fill that void. If you need to understand or become familiar with topics or procedures in which you have little experience, once again, graduate school will fill that space. It takes time to gain experience in your field of interest before you pursue a graduate degree.

Look for Opportunities to Publish

There are very few students who publish; this could be as simple as an article in the college newspaper to an academic journal article. What would set you apart from other job candidates is to have on your résumé that you have published in your field of expertise. If at all possible, connect with a professor in your field of choice and pursue writing for publication. This will give you credibility and will help you stand out to employers and job recruiters.

Stay Abreast of the News

College students have so much to do and little time to incorporate everything they have to do and do it well. Now, add staying abreast of the news to that list. The reasons to know what is going on in the world and close to home are many. First, you are considered an educated person once you graduate. With this diploma come certain expectations such as knowledge of the world and your surroundings. Second, you'll be able to talk intelligently to upper management and your peers on subjects such as politics, economics, and foreign policy, for example. Finally, you will be able to talk comfortably and confidently at networking events, parties, and functions you attend.

The news offers information that can help you personally. There are articles on the economy, job search strategies, fashion, theatre, and so on. You'll have so much information to share that networking will become very easy to do.

The easiest way to get the news every day is to listen to the radio or TV one hour a day. The more you get interested in staying abreast of the news, the more you want to hear the news. It is an addictive process. Also, the Internet provides a variety of sources for daily news stories. Scanning the top news stories each day does not take much time and you'll see that staying abreast of the news is very beneficial.

THE CAREER PLANNING PROCESS

Do you have an answer to the question, "What are you going to do when you graduate?" If you have followed the suggestions in the book, the question is not as overwhelming as when you began. There is a system to finding a job: a good job. And, you can learn to work the system. By checking off some of the many tasks associated with finding a job, you have paved the way through college to career. If after you graduate, the job you seek is not attained, take the pressure off yourself as you navigate the system to eventually find a job that you want. You have the tools and techniques.

Good luck and enjoy the journey!

Appendix A

General Websites

APTITUDE AND ASSESSMENT TESTS

Online Career Assessment Tools
Review for Job-Seekers, Career-Seekers

www.quintcareers.com/online_
assessment_review.html

Self-assessment resources

www.rileyguide.com/assess.html

GENERAL WEBSITES

Job search website for articles and
information on the job search

www.job-hunt.org

The Riley Guide career and research
center; includes job descriptions, salary
data, and employment statistics

www.rileyguide.com

Toronto Public Library career and job
search help blog

http://torontopubliclibrary.
typepad.com/jobhelp

The *Wall Street Journal* careers

www.careerjournal.com

Weddle's; sign up for free newsletter
for job seekers and career activists

www.weddles.com/seekernews/
index.cfm

This website offers career information
on mayor industries

www.wetfeet.com

Quintessential Careers is a guide to
researching companies and industries

www.quintcareers.com

Detailed information on more than 50,000 companies	www.hoovers.com
A primary source for employee directors within companies	www.jigsaw.com
A searchable directory of nonprofit organizations	www2.guidestar.org
A database of ranked listing of companies, people, and resources	www.specialissues.com/lol
Fortune Magazine's list of the best companies to work for	http://money.cnn.com/magazines/ fortune/bestcompanies/2013 (updated annually)

OCCUPATION/CAREER LISTINGS

This website offers links on employment trends, labor market information, etc.	www.khake.com/page5.html
The Riley Guide career and research center; includes job descriptions, salary data, and employment statistics	www.rileyguide.com
This website adds statistics for industries and provides information on job trends	www.Indeed.com
This website is an online version of the *Occupational Outlook Handbook*, which includes career information on training, education, salaries, and wages for all types of occupations	www.bls.gov/oco
This online website is similar to the *Occupational Outlook Handbook*, as it provides information on careers by industry	www.bls.gov/oco/cg
Occupational Outlook Quarterly is an online magazine covering topics such as occupations and training opportunities	www.bls.gov/opub/ooq/ ooqhome.htm

The Occupational Information Network or O*Net Online is an online occupations database sponsored by the U.S. Department of Labor/Employment and Training Administration	http://online.onetcenter.org
An online listing of associations by profession and industry	www.weddles.com/associations/index.cfm

OTHER WEBSITES OF NOTE

The Classifieds News Blog posts an annual ranking of the top 15 U.S. job search websites	http://blog.daype.com/tips/top-us-job-search-websites.html
Free résumé, cover letter, etc. site	http://susanireland.com
Free help on career advancement	http://dalekurow.com
Free information on career help	www.acinet.org
Career guidance	www.humanworkplace.com
Newspapers/magazines *Wall Street Journal* *Fortune* *Fast Company* *Forbes*	http://online.wsj.com/home-page http://money.cnn.com/magazines/fortune/ www.fastcompany.com www.forbes.com
Ten ways to use LinkedIn	http://blog.guykawasaki.com/2007/01/ten_ways_to_use.html#axzz0nAh7w5bx
Employees post reviews of the companies they work for	www.glassdoor.com www.vault.com

Appendix B

Associations to Join by Major

ACCOUNTING AND FINANCE

- *American Bankers Association*: Founded in 1875, the American Bankers Association represents banks of all sizes, supporting the nation's banking industry and employees.
- *The American Finance Association (AFA)*: The purpose of the American Finance Association is to promote the knowledge of financial economics.
- *American Society of Women Accountants (ASWA)*: The ASWA, formed in 1938, provides opportunities for women in all fields of accounting and finance.
- *Association for Financial Professionals, Inc. (AFP)*: The AFP serves treasury and finance professionals.
- *International Federation of Accountants (IFAC)*: IFAC is a global organization, representing 2.5 million accountants employed.
- *National Association of Black Accountants*: Since 1969, this group has strived to promote and develop minority professionals in the fields of accounting and finance.
- *The Professional Accounting Society of America (PASA)*: Since 2005, PASA has focused on entry-level and mid-level associates working at accounting firms across America.
- *American Institute of CPAs (AICPA)*
- *Chartered Institute of Management Accountants (CIMA)*
- *National Society of Accountants*

117

- *American Accounting Society*
- *Boomer Knowledge Network (online community of accounting firms)*

BUSINESS MANAGEMENT AND SUPPLY CHAIN MANAGEMENT

- *American Management Association (AMA)*: The AMA provides trainings and valuable resources to ensure business professionals stay knowledgeable in the competitive business world.
- *American Production and Inventory Control Society (APICS)*: The APICS provides research and education and certification programs for supply chain and operations management professionals.
- *DECA*: This international, nonprofit organization has been developing the business skills of college and high school students since 1946. *DECA members have the opportunity* to network with local business leaders and develop business skills through mock presentations and competitions.
- *Entrepreneurs' Organization*: The Entrepreneurs' Organization is a global network working to enhance entrepreneurs' abilities to be successful by learning and growing from each other's knowledge and experience.

CRIMINAL JUSTICE

- California Criminalistics Institute
- The American Academy of Forensic Science
- Association of Government Accountants
- National Criminal Justice Association (NCJA)
- Academy of Criminal Justice Sciences
- American Jail Association
- Association for Criminal Justice Research
- National Center for Victims of Crime
- International Association of Directors of Law Enforcement Standards and Training
- American Bar Association

ENTREPRENEURSHIP

- Haas Entrepreneur Association
- Venture Capital Roundtable
- The Entrepreneur Roundtable

GLOBAL LOGISTICS

- The International Society of Logistics (SOLE)
- Global Coalition for Efficient Logistics (GCEL)
- American Society of Transportation and Logistics (ASTL)

HEALTH CARE MANAGEMENT

- *American Association of Healthcare Administrative Management (AAHAM)*: AAHAM is the premier professional organization in health care administrative management. It's become a resource for information, education, and advocacy on issues and trends in health care management.
- *The Professional Association of Health Care Office Management*: This association is designed to focus on local health care concerns by networking with hospitals and medical organizations to help solve local problems.

HUMAN RESOURCES

- *The International Association of Administrative Professionals (IAAP)*: Founded in 1942, the IAAP provides administrative professionals opportunities for growth, networking, education, and development.
- *National Human Resources Association (NHRA)*: The NHRA was established in 1961 to support the professional development of human resource professionals.
- *Professionals in Human Resources Association (PIHRA)*: Founded in 1944, the PIHRA provides human resources professionals the opportunity to collaborate in an effort to enhance the profession.
- *The Society for Human Resource Management (SHRM)*: SHRM is the world's largest human resources (HR) membership association and is dedicated to serving the needs of HR managers.

INFORMATION SYSTEMS

- Association for Information Systems
- Information Systems Security Association

MANAGEMENT

- California Management Association
- International Professional Managers Association
- Project Management Institute

MARKETING

- *American Marketing Association (AMA)*: The AMA is the largest marketing association in North America and is a resource that thousands of marketers utilize daily.
- *eMarketing Association (eMA)*: The eMA is the world's largest international association of eMarketing professionals, providing resources and services to the online marketing community.
- *The National Association of Sales Professionals (NASP)*: Since 1991, the NASP has been committed to developing sales professionals to become leaders in the ever-evolving sales world.
- *Sales and Marketing Executives International (SMEI)*: SMEI is the worldwide organization dedicated to connecting individuals in the sales and marketing arenas.
- *Social Media Club*: Social Media Club is a professional organization that promotes social media literacy. They work to develop industry standards and provide members knowledge of industry trends in the cutting-edge field of social media marketing.

PUBLIC ADMINISTRATION

- Public Administration Theory Network
- Eastern Regional Organization for Public Administration
- Commonwealth Association for Public Administration and Management

Appendix C

The Aspirational Résumé

Aspirational Résumé: *tutorial example*

Name: Jane Student

OBJECTIVE

What kind of opportunity am I looking for?

A teacher in biological sciences and eventually a forensic science teacher.

Where do you want to be in 4–5 years?

I hope to graduate from the California State University Dominguez Hills, majoring in biology and pursue a graduate degree in science. My specific field after graduation is unknown at this time.

What do you need to do to get there?

In order for me to get there, I need to: graduate college, build experience, obtain internships, and network.

EDUCATION

Bachelor of Science degree: Biology, June 2019

Minor: Criminal Justice Administration

California State University, Dominguez Hills

Relevant Coursework: Biology, Chemistry, Anatomy

Study Abroad: I do not plan to study abroad throughout my undergraduate college years.

RELEVANT EXPERIENCE

Mayfair High School   2017–2021

Carson, California   90747

Student Teacher

- Assist in classrooms in all teaching-related activities
- Teach one semester supervised by a credentialed teacher

California State University, Dominguez Hills   2016–2017

Carson, California   90747

Associated Students, Inc. Associate

- Build individual and group leadership skills through leading projects and fundraisers
- Advocate on behalf of students of the university on political and university issues

MEMBERSHIPS AND CLUBS

What on-campus clubs am I interested in pursuing?

- Associated Students Incorporated
- Biology Club

What professional organizations are there in my field?

- National Science Teachers' Association
- The National Education Society
- The National Association of Biology Teachers

PERSONAL NOTES/IDEAS

People have suggested that I explore options in my first year of college. Also, people suggested joining clubs.

Résumé, Cover Letter, and Stellar References Examples

Brent A. Vaughan

bvaughan@company.com   Office: (626) 555-5555
bvaughan@yahoo.com   Mobile: (626) 555-5555

OBJECTIVE

Seeking an Office Manager position utilizing appropriate methods and a flexible interpersonal style to help ensure the effective and efficient flow of work throughout the office.

SUMMARY OF QUALIFICATIONS

- Over 8 years' experience in office management
- Proficient in MS Word/Excel/PowerPoint/Publisher/Outlook
- Skilled in technical writing, including proposals, user manuals, and documentation
- Bilingual in English and Spanish

EDUCATION

California State University, Dominguez Hills   June 2011
Bachelor of Arts Degree, Major: Business Administration
Concentration: Business Information Systems
Major GPA: 3.6 (4.0 = A)

PROFESSIONAL WORK EXPERIENCE

TELLER COMMUNICATIONS, Dallas, Texas   *2004–PRESENT*
OFFICE MANAGER
- Create and manage office work schedules/hours and implement adjustments due to customer needs.
- Prepare recommendations for an annual budget prior to each fiscal year and compare budget to actual performance.
- Handle and mediate Human Resource issues and employee problem resolutions by communicating effectively with managers, supervisors, and employees.
- Negotiate the purchase of office supplies and office equipment in accordance with company purchasing policies and budgetary restrictions.
- Maintain clean, professional, and safe working environment by inspecting and scheduling maintenance; ensure office and warehouse equipment is properly accounted for and in safe working condition.
- Ensure participation of all associates in all corporate orientation and training programs.

GRAYSON ELECTRONICS, DALLAS, TEXAS   *2001–2004*

OFFICE MANAGER

- Planned and monitored daily staffing schedules and adjusted accordingly to ensure adequate staffing levels that support operational demands and business objectives.
- Maintained and updated departmental policies and procedures manual.
- Managed and oversaw administrative functions to ensure all paperwork was processed efficiently and in a timely manner.
- Researched opportunities for improved services to clients, presented ideas to CEO and had 5 new policies implemented.
- Reviewed clerical and personnel records to ensure accuracy of data.
- Created training materials and led workshops to assist with employee development based on needs expressed by department supervisors.

MARK TWO DESIGNS, AUSTIN, TEXAS   *1999–2001*

ADMINISTRATIVE ASSISTANT

- Analyzed and organized office operations and procedures such as preparation of payroll, information management/filing systems, requisition of supplies and other clerical services.
- Established uniform correspondence procedures and style practices.
- Monitored and controlled overtime and associates' absences; submitted payroll timely and accurately.
- Ensured safety methods, practices and programs were implemented and maintained by monitoring effectiveness every 6 months.
- Formulated procedures for systematic retention, protection, retrieval, transfer, and disposal of records.

CERTIFICATIONS

- Project Management Professional Certification (PMP), Project Management Institute, 2001

AFFILIATIONS

- Academy of Management (Member)
- Project Management Institute (Member)
- Women In Technology (Member)

Brent A. Vaughan

bvaughan@company.com   Office: (626) 555-5555
bvaughan@yahoo.com   Mobile: (626) 555-5555

August 12, 2010

Dr. Andy Mann
Project Manager
Ohm R. Avery, Inc.
11 Orange Grove Avenue
Pasadena, CA 91125

Dear Dr. Mann:

In your opening paragraph, state how you learned about the position. If you heard about the
position from someone who works for the organization, be sure to mention his/her name,
department, etc. Give a brief introduction of yourself and your background. Explain your
interests that match the job description and the organization. Why do you want to work for this
particular organization?

In the second paragraph (and third if necessary) illustrate how your experiences align with the
job description. This could include work, school, volunteer, church, etc. experience. Use
specific language stated in the job description! Your task is to make it easy for the employer to
see a match between you and the job. Why should the organization ask you in for an interview?

In the last paragraph state that you will contact them! Be proactive and give a date that you will
contact them if you have not heard from them first. Express your appreciation to the person who
you are directing the letter to and your eagerness to discuss the employment opportunity.

Sincerely,

Brent Vaughan

Brent A. Vaughan

bvaughan@company.com   Office: (626) 555-5555
bvaughan@yahoo.com   Mobile: (626) 555-5555

REFERENCES

Kathy Doroger
CFO, Albertsons
kdoroger@albertsons.com
Business: 805-898-4576
Mobile: 805-637-2424

Karl Ponto
Manager, Albertsons
kponto@yahoo.com
4356 Brockton Avenue #33
Los Angeles, CA 90025
Business: 310-999-3456

Janet Olstead
Financial Analyst, Ralphs Grocery Co.
Janetolstead@gmail.com
1304 E. Charles Street
Pasadena, CA 91104
Business: 626-454-3344
Mobile: 323-610-3456

Linda Jones
Financial Analyst, Taco Bell
lindajones@tbell.com
4444 Shoreline Drive
Portland, Oregon 97333

Appendix E

Interview Preparation

Questions you may be asked in the interview:
1. Tell me about yourself.
2. What do you know about our company?
3. Why should we hire you?
4. What do you look for in a job?
5. How would your colleagues describe you?
6. How would your boss describe you?
7. How would you describe yourself?
8. Name one significant accomplishment in your last position.
9. Describe a difficult issue/situation and how you solved it.
10. What are your career goals? Where do you see yourself in five years?
11. What are your strong points?
12. What are your weak areas?
13. How did you do in school?
14. What questions didn't I ask that you expected?
15. Do you have any questions for me?

Questions you may want to ask the interviewer (only if not already discussed during the interview):
1. Who will be my immediate supervisor?
2. What will my duties be?
3. Tell me what it is like working here in terms of the people, management practices, workloads, expected performance, and rewards.
4. What training is available for this position?
5. What is the organizational structure, and where does this position fit in?
6. What are the major challenges for the person in this position?

7. What do you like best about working for this company/organization?
8. Is travel required for this position?
9. How is job performance evaluated?
10. May I have a tour of the facilities?

Bibliography

Astin, A. W., Parrot, S., Korn, W., & Sax, L. (1997). *The American freshman—Thirty year trends, 1966–1996.* Los Angeles, CA: Higher Education Research Institute.

Beatty, R. (2000). *The resume kit* (4th ed.). New York, NY: John Wiley & Sons, Inc.

Brooks, K. (2010). *You majored in what? Mapping your path from chaos to career.* New York, NY: Penguin Group.

Carroll, L. (1865). *Alice's adventures in Wonderland.* London, England: Macmillan.

Cuseo, J. (2005). Decided, undecided, and in transition: Implications for advisement, career counseling, and student retention. In R. S. Feldman (Ed.), *Improving the first year of college: Research and practice* (pp. 27–50). New York, NY: Erlbaum.

Deresiewicz, W. (2014, July 21). Don't send your kid to the Ivy League, the nation's top colleges are turning our kids into zombies. *The New Republic.* Retrieved from: https://newrepublic.com/article/118747/ivy-league-schools-are-overrated-send-your-kids-elsewhere.

Dyer, W. (2004). *The power of intention: Learning to co-create your world your way.* Carlsbad, CA: Hay House.

Ferrazzi, K. (2005). *Never eat alone.* New York, NY: Doubleday.

Graber, S. (2000). *The everything cover letter book.* Holbrook, MA: Adams Media Corporation.

Glass, A., & Brody, M. (2006). *You can't do it alone: Building relationships for career success.* Jenkintown, PA: Career Skills Press.

Gordon, V. (1994). *Issues in advising the undecided college student.* Columbia: University of South Carolina, National Resource Center for the Freshman Year Experience.

Gordon, V. N. (1995). *The undecided college student: An academic and career advising challenge* (2nd ed.). Springfield, IL: C.C. Thomas.

Greene, S., & Martel, M. (2012). *The ultimate job searcher's guidebook.* South-Western Mason, OH: Cengage Learning.

Higgins, M. C. (2000). The more, the merrier? Multiple developmental relationships and work satisfaction. *The Journal of Management Development, 19,* 277–296.

Jensen, B. (2005). *What is your life's work?* New York, NY: Harper Collins Publishers, Inc.

Kram, K. E. (1988). *Mentoring at work: Developmental relationships in organizational life.* Lanham, MD: University Press of America.

Lewallen, W. C. (1993). The impact of being "undecided" on college student persistence. *Journal of College Student Development, 34*, 103–112.

Lewallen, W. C. (1995). Students decided and undecided about career choice: A comparison of college achievement and student involvement. *NACADA Journal, 15*(1), 22–30.

McDonald, M., & Steele, G. E. (2007). Adapting learning theory to advising first-year undecided students. In M. S. Hunter, B. McCalla-Wriggins, & E. R. White (Eds.), *Academic advising: New insights for teaching and learning in the first year* (pp. 185–201). Columbia: University of South Carolina, National Resource Center for the First-Year Experience and Students in Transition.

Micceri, T. (2002, May 30). *Will changing your major double your graduation chances?* Invited paper posted on the First-Year Assessment Listserv, sponsored by the Policy Center for the First Year of College.

Musselman, J. (2005). *The hip girl's handbook for the working world.* Tulsa, OK: Wildcat Canyon Press.

National Association of Colleges and Employers. (2015, 2013). *Job outlook 2015, 2013.* Bethlehem, PA: Author. Retrieved from http://www.naceweb.org

National Commission on Writing. (2004). *Writing: A ticket to work ... or a ticket out: A survey of business leaders.* Retrieved from the College Board website: http://www.collegeboard.com/prod_downloads/writingcom/writing-ticket-to-work.pdf

Noel, L., & Levitz, R. (1995). New strategies for difficult times. *Recruitment & Retention in Higher Education, 9*(7), 4–7.

Pinker, S. (2014, September 4). The trouble with Harvard: The Ivy League is broken and only standardized tests can fix it. *The New Republic.* Retrieved from: https://newrepublic.com/article/119321/harvard-ivy-league-should-judge-students-standardized-tests.

Pollak, L. (2012). *Getting from college to career: Your essential guide to succeeding in the real world.* New York, NY: Harper Business.

Rampy, L. M. (2009). *Build your network and get it working for you.* Presentation at Project Management Institute—Los Angeles Chapter meeting.

Reeves, E. (2009). *Can I wear my nose ring to the interview?* New York, NY: Workman.

Rogers, J. (2012). *Coaching skills: A handbook* (3rd ed.). New York, NY: McGraw-Hill.

Rogers, J., Witteworth, K., & Gilbert, A. (2008). *The manager as coach. The new way to get results* (2nd ed.). New York, NY: McGraw-Hill.

Stanier, M. (2010). *Do more great work.* New York, NY: Workman.

Teller, E. (2008). *Developmental networks and their impact on the careers of women in information technology.* Fielding Graduate University Santa Barbara, CA: Dissertation.

U.S. Department of Labor. (2014). Retrieved from www.dol.gov/odep/topics/youth/softskills/Networking.pdf.

About the Author

Vera Teller is currently on staff at California State University Dominguez Hills as a lecturer in the College of Business Administration and Public Policy. Her professional career spans over 25 years' experience in business, management, and information systems as director of Systems and Programming for Safeway (Vons) and Trader Joe's, consultant for EDS, and program manager for WellPoint.

Vera holds a PhD and MA from the Fielding Graduate University in Human and Organization Development, an MBA from California State University, Los Angeles, specializing in business information systems, and has certification from University of California, Los Angeles (UCLA) in data communications, microcomputer, and LAN support. Vera obtained her Project Management Professional certification in 2000 from the Project Management Institute.

Vera's interest in career advancement opportunities in the information technology (IT) field is based on personal and professional experience. She extensively researched networks and their impact on women's careers. She has been a speaker for Pasadena Community TV Channel 56 on unemployment issues. She also spoke at the Project Management Institute chapter conferences, Business Analysts conference, Los Angeles Quality Assurance conference, and Chinese American IT conference on societal factors that created barriers to women advancing in the workplace.

Vera serves on the Executive Committee as secretary for Women At Work, a nonprofit organization helping all people reach their full employment and earning potential. Vera wrote and managed the strategic planning process for 2011–2014.

Vera lives in Bell Canyon, California, with her husband. She has two children, a daughter-in-law, two adorable grandchildren and a third grandchild due the end of August 2016.